Zá-to-pek! Zá-to-pek! Zá-to-pek!

THE LIFE AND TIMES OF THE WORLD'S GREATEST DISTANCE RUNNER

by Bob Phillips

WITH CONTRIBUTIONS FROM ROBERTO QUERCETANI, COLIN YOUNG, MEL WATMAN AND NEIL ALLEN

STATISTICAL SUMMARY BY MILAN SKOCOVSKÝ & STANISLAV HRNCÍR

The Parrs Wood Press
MANCHESTER

First Published 2002
Revised and re-printed 2004

THE PARRS WOOD PRESS
St Wilfrid's Enterprise Centre
Royce Road, Manchester, M15 5BJ
www.parrswoodpress.com

© Bob Phillips 2002

ISBN: 1 903158 25 7

Printed and bound in Spain

CONTENTS

PHOTOGRAPHS

(between pages 80 and 81)

FOREWORD

By Roberto Quercetani

Laying the firm foundations of "The Zátopek Era"

I AM AMONG the lucky track fans who saw Emil Zátopek in his "Week of Weeks" at the Helsinki Olympics in 1952, and about a quarter-of-a-century later I met up with him during the European Championships in Prague in 1978. I found him to be as kind and humorous as ever, even though he had gone through troubled times for those who turned out to be the temporary losers during the Prague Spring of 1968.

I invited him to give me his retrospective views on his track career, and what he said in reply was, in fact, a monument to his proverbial modesty. In sharp contrast to the type of champion from yesteryear who likes to take refuge in the ivory tower of his "old days", he candidly told me that he thought that he had had a fair amount of luck. Competition then was not as intense, he said. Most countries still had to heal the wounds caused by the Second World War. The turnover in talent was slow, and Finland's great runners had disappeared, apart from Viljo Heino, and even he was nearing the end of his career.

Recalling the 1952 Olympic marathon, when he won his third gold medal of the Games, Zátopek said that it was probably his easiest victory. It was not the "new" distance that frightened him but rather the possibility of a particularly fast pace - and nobody chose to impose that on him. This checks with the story that while sharing the lead in the race Zátopek, the novice, is said to have addressed his companions - Gustaf Jansson, of Sweden, and Jim Peters, of Great Britain - with the following words in English: "I know virtually nothing about marathon running, but do you think we ought to go a little faster?" Receiving no answer, he quickened the pace and ran away from his rivals.

Already in 1946, when he was 5th in the European Championships 5000 metres as a virtual unknown, Zátopek was laying the foundations of a new era in distance running - "The Zátopek Era" - and his competitive achievements can only be fully appreciated if you are able to view them in the context of those byegone years, rather than from a present-day perspective. The same applies to his training loads, which half-a-century ago were considered to be among the heaviest ever tried until then by top-class distance runners.

Yet if valued in terms of quantity his feats may still be unparalleled. In his day European athletes competed in a large number of meetings at club and national level and in international dual matches, and I can quote some figures from his career which aptly tell the tale. During 1949 Zátopek ran the 10,000 metres on 11 occasions in competition over a period of no more than 134 days. In 1950 he ran 20 races at 5000 metres in 161 days. The greatest distance-runner of the present era, Haile Gebrselassie, usually runs no more than two or three races a year at either of these distances.

Zátopek's winning sequences were also very impressive. He was undefeated at 5000 and 10,000 metres from October 1948 to June 1952 - a total of 72 races! He did not lose a race at 10,000 metres for more than six years from May 1948 to July 1954, with 38 successive wins! In the more heated atmosphere of present-day competition Gebrselassie has been able to remain unscathed for an even longer period of time, while obviously being more cautious in choosing his meetings. At 5000 metres he could point to 16 consecutive wins from August 1995 to the end of the year 2000, while at 10,000 metres his winning "streak" had lasted seven years but covered only 11 races.

On the occasion that I met Zátopek in 1978 he gave me a drawing which he had done himself, showing him being hotly pursued by his wife, Dana, with a javelin in her hand, and as we well know they have established a record between them which may never be equalled. They were astrological twins, born on the same day (19 September 1922), and they won Olympic gold medals on the same day (24 July 1952).

As a champion distance-runner Emil Zátopek had no weaknesses. A superlative solo runner who received little or no help from others in his record attempts, he was also a clever tactician and an almost unbeatable finisher. He never revealed great potential as a middle-distance runner, and yet his sudden bursts of speed accounted for numerous victims.

FOREWORD

Last but not least, he was a supreme fighter. The year 1954 marked the beginning of the end for this fantastic human machine. He had shown the way, and others quickly followed in his footsteps, taking upon themselves a similar burden of daily sacrifices. Yet at the age of 31 he still rose to the challenge magnificently and ran faster than ever before over both 5000 and 10,000 metres.

Dr Roberto Quercetani is recognised as the World's foremost authority on athletics. He has followed the sport passionately ever since his childhood in the early 1930s in his native Italy and has contributed articles to newspapers and magazines in many countries for more than 50 years. He was a founder member of the Association of Track & Field Statisticians in 1950 and was for many years editor of the "World Sports" International Athletics Annual. He is also, most notably, the author of the definitive study of the sport, "Athletics: A History of Modern Track & Field Athletics", of which the latest edition was published by SEP Editrice sri (Milan) in the year 2000.

PREFACE

By Bob Phillips

In fondest memory of the truly greatest
of distance-runners

SOME 40 YEARS of working in journalism and in public relations should have taught me, I suppose, that categorical claims about almost any matter under the sun are hazardous in the extreme. Yet I did not hesitate over-long in describing the late Emil Zátopek in the sub-title to this book as "the World's Greatest Distance Runner", even knowing as I tapped the words out on the keyboard that there would be those potential readers who would bridle at the idea that anyone from a long gone era could possibly be compared with the great African athletes who have astounded and delighted us over recent years - particularly, of course, Haile Gebrselassie.

It's an interesting thought that Gebrselassie, though from the most contrasting of cultures, is a very similar character to Zátopek. Both of them, despite their vastly different cultural upbringing, have brought a serene and eminently approachable manner to the serious business of winning gold medals and breaking World records, and often they have done so in some marked contrast to tighter-lipped opponents. But then the most eminent of the current generation of distance-runners have had to become accustomed to the idea of being regularly beaten by Gebrselassie, just as their predecessors were required to yield so often to Zátopek some half-a-century earlier, so the vanquished multitude perhaps has good reason for being less cheery of disposition.

I had actually wanted to write this book several years ago when Emil, though failing in health, was still with us, but involvement with other projects set the schedule back, and then we were saddened by the news of his death in November 2000. So this work has become a tribute *in memoriam* but is actually little different in structure to what I had originally planned. I had started out with the intention of making a close study of Emil's training and racing regime, based on the best available contemporary

8

PREFACE

accounts and interviews, and that is what I have still done. Some very long-established friends in athletics - Neil Allen, Roberto Quercetani, Mel Watman and Colin Young - have done me the honour of adding their thoughts and recollections in separate contributions, while the leading Czech statisticians, Milan Skocovský and Stanislav Hrncír, have compiled the most comprehensive list yet published of Zátopek's races, and elsewhere you will find the observations of other athletics experts (and passionate devotees) such as David Thurlow, Stan Greenberg and Peter Lovesey.

Among others to whose authoritative reports on Zátopek's activities I have made frequent references are the twins, Norris and Ross McWhirter, whose monthly magazine, 'Athletics World', was such an outstanding chronicle of the sport in the 1950s; and the late P.W. ("Jimmy") Green and J. Armour Milne, who as Editor and East European correspondent respectively of 'Athletics Weekly' wrote profusely about Zátopek. The comprehensive and graphic collection of photographs published here was ably researched by Dave Terry, whose sports library is second to none. I am grateful to them all.

Bob Phillips,
Boutières, France, July 2004

The author is the editor of "Track Stats", the quarterly publication of the National Union of Track Statisticians which covers all historical and statistical aspects of the sport. His book, "Honour of Empire, Glory of Sport", published in the year 2000 and relating the history of athletics at the Commonwealth Games, was selected by "The Times" as one of its Sports Books of the Year. He has also written a biography of Bill Roberts, the British Olympic relay gold-medallist from 1936, and his history of the mile race, "3:59.4: The Quest for the Four-Minute Mile", was published in 2004. He was a member of the BBC Radio commentary team for 17 years and has attended all the major Championships during that time. He began his modest competitive career as a sprinter and finished it 36 years later as a marathon runner and then took up time-trial cycle racing.

1.

INTRODUCTION

Why should it be a Czech named Emil?
Why not, instead, a Swede named Bertil?

HAD IT BEEN A Finn who became the World's greatest distance runner in the late 1940s, no one would have been the least surprised. After all, it had been the Finns who had won 10 of the 12 Olympic gold medals at 5,000 and 10,000 metres from 1912 to 1936 and who had set 14 of the 15 World records at those distances during the years up to 1948.

If it had been a Swede, instead, it would not have taken unawares those who considered themselves to be in the know. Though the wartime record-breaking exploits of Hägg and Andersson had very largely centred on the 1500-to-3000 metres range, Hägg had run an historic sub-14 minutes for 5000 metres in a rare serious involvement with the event in 1942 at the age of 23, and the premature end to which his career was brought because of infringement of the rules concerning amateurism could well have been seen as merely opening up opportunities for another of his talented fellow-countrymen.

If a Frenchman had emerged as the World leader, memories would have been fondly evoked of Guillemot, the Olympic champion at 5,000 metres in 1920, and Bouin, the World record-breaker at 10,000 metres from before the First World War. A pretender from Poland would have been welcomed as the natural successor to Kusocinski, the Olympic 10,000 metres winner over the Flying Finns in 1932 and maybe also the inventor of interval training. Even an American - perhaps realising the untapped Transatlantic potential personified by the Los Angeles 5,000 metres silver-medallist, Ralph Hill - would not have seemed out of place on the Wembley Olympic rostrum in 1948 or claiming his IAAF record-breaking plaques.

INTRODUCTION

Perhaps it could have been a Briton who would have at long last transformed a much-lauded cross-country heritage into something of rather greater international significance. Maybe the Soviet Union would have revealed an unexpected talent in the footsteps of the Znamenskiy brothers from the late 1930s. It could even conceivably have been a South American in the wake of Zabala, the marathon champion of 1932. No one, of course, would have given any thought at all in the 1940s to the prospects of candidates from many other parts of the World - from Africa, from Australasia, from Asia, even from much of Europe. There simply were not any.

A Czech was as unimaginable a contender as a Cherokee Indian or a Chinaman. Where was Czechoslovakia's legacy? What possible inspiration was there to be found in such an obscure corner of Central Europe?

No pioneering statistician of the era such as Quercetani or Potts, however diligently he searched through the record-books, could possibly have hypothesised that the ancient Empire of Moravia would be birthplace to one of the very greatest athletes of the century. There had been a Czech named Oskar Hekš who had finished a perfectly respectable 8th in the 1932 Olympic marathon. Further delving would have unearthed a 16th place for another Czech in that same event in 1928 and a couple of 17th places at 10,000 metres. None of this, though, could have been interpreted as any sort of evidence of a trend or a tradition.

To judge by the Finnish example, distance runners ought to come forward to the front ranks only by dint of Nordic stoicism and perseverance over the fulness of time as their predecessors stepped aside, willingly or otherwise. Heino, in 1944, had followed Mäki, from 1938-39, just as Mäki had taken after Salminen, from 1937, and Lehtinen, from 1932. Lehtinen and then Salminen, in their turn, had succeeded Nurmi and Ritola, from the 1920s. Nurmi and Ritola had assumed the place of Kolehmainen, from 1912.

This all had a very satisfying logical progression to it, and when peacetime returned to Europe in 1945 there seemed no reason to doubt that Viljo Heino would carry on the natural Finnish succession. The previous year he had run 10,000 metres in 29min 35.4sec to beat Mäki's World record by 17.2sec - a greater margin of progress than anyone else had achieved since Nurmi in 1921. At the 1946 European

ZÁ-TO-PEK! ZÁ-TO-PEK! ZÁ-TO-PEK!

Championships in Oslo Heino won the same event by a very large margin in the second fastest time ever of 29:52.0, and it was another Finn who had finished 2nd.

Admittedly, at 5,000 metres in those Championships Heino had placed only 4th, a long way behind the British winner, Wooderson, but this race took place the day after the 10,000 and Heino could be excused on the grounds of inadequate time for recovery. Some small but rather more significant sign ought to have been remarked upon that Heino, at 32, and Perälä, the 10,000 metres silver-medallist a year his junior, were comparative veterans by the criteria of that age, as was Wooderson. Much younger were the other Oslo medallists at 5,000 metres: Slijkhuis, of Holland, and Nyberg, of Sweden, were both in their early 20s.

The results of those first two major Championship distance races to be held on the track since 1938 were as follows :

5000 metres: 1 Wooderson (GB) 14:08.6, 2 Slijkhuis (Holland) 14:14.0, 3 Nyberg (Sweden) 14:23.2, 4 Heino (Finland) 14:24.4, 5 Zátopek (Czechoslovakia) 14:25.8, 6 Reiff (Belgium) 14:45.8, 7 Greenfort (Denmark) 14:46.0, 8 Pujazon (France) 14:46.8, 9 Breistroffer (France) 14:50.4, 10 Poulsen (Denmark) 14:53.6, 11 Heirendt (Luxemburg) 15:00.6, 12 van de Wattyne (Belgium) 15:08.0, 13 Pataki (Hungary) 15:33.6, 14 Aasbo (Norway) 15:33.8. Did not finish: Dawonkowski (Poland), Perälä (Finland), Durkfeldt (Sweden), Rohne (Norway).

10,000 metres: 1 Heino (Finland) 29:52.0, 2 Perälä (Finland) 30:31.4, 3 Csaplár (Hungary) 30:35.2, 4 Rapp (Sweden) 30:49.2, 5 Vanin (USSR) 30:56.2, 6 Heirendt (Luxemburg) 31:08.2, 7 Wilhelmsen (Norway) 31:20.8, 8 Stokken (Norway) 32:56.0. Did not finish: Tillman (Sweden), Beviacqua (Italy).

Of the 20 fastest in the World at 5000 metres in 1946, 15 were either Finnish or Swedish. Of the 20 fastest at 10,000 metres, 13 were either Finnish or Swedish. Even so, Slijkhuis and the Belgian, Reiff, who was 25, both ran 8:08.8 for 3000 metres during the year in separate races, and although Hägg's World record of 8:01.2 was still a long way ahead it was no longer unassailable.

12

INTRODUCTION

Swedish runners, in the majestic manner of Hägg and Anderssson, had monopolised the Oslo 1500 metres - Strand 1st in 3:48.0, Eriksson 2nd in 3:48.8, a Dane 3rd a long way behind in 3:52.8 - and that was a result which might have prompted the keenest students of the sport to muse that as Strand, Eriksson and the European 800 metres champion, Gustafsson, were the three fastest Swedes at the distance then any one of the six others from the same country who also ranked in the World's top dozen at 1500 metres might reasonably consider that their future lay at a longer distance. Why not, for example, a 24-year-old named Bertil Albertsson, who had run 3:51.4 for 1500 metres (9th in the World), 14:41.8 for 5000 metres (25th) and 30:51.8 for 10,000 metres (7th)? There was clearly plenty of room for advancement in his case.

We all know now, of course, that it was the Czech, Emil Zátopek, rather than a Slijkhuis, a Reiff or an Albertsson, who was to revolutionise the whole concept of distance running in the years which followed, having occupied a highly commendable but largely disregarded 5th place in the Oslo 5,000 metres at the age of 23. In the half-century and more until his death, much has been written about Zátopek, his races and his training, and yet there still remains something of a mystery as to why it should have been he, and not somebody else more obviously qualified, who displayed the indomitable spirit and the inexhaustible physical resources which led to so many unprecedented achievements.

There may yet be another athlete to come who will break more records in more events than Zátopek. There may even be someone superior to Gebrselassie, winner of six Olympic and World titles at 10,000 metres, who will obtain three gold medals in distance events at an Olympics, however unlikely that may seem. There will be those who will argue that Gebrselassie has faced more intensive competition from a much wider spectrum of the globe than Zátopek ever did, and that therefore Gebrselassie must be the better athlete.

Certainly, the respective merits of the two runners will forever be a subject for fervent debate among those with a feeling for the history of the sport, but this is all of no more than academic interest. Is Alexander the Great superior to the Duke of Wellington? Shakespeare to Chekhov? John Donne to Ezra Pound? Botticelli to Georges Seurat? Buddy Bolden to Miles Davis?

ZÁ-TO-PEK! ZÁ-TO-PEK! ZÁ-TO-PEK!

The fact is that in chronological terms Zátopek came first. His most renowned racing strategy - taking the lead, constantly forcing the pace to unsettle his pursuers - was the antithesis of Nurmi and his dictatorial stopwatch. No one before Zátopek had dared attempt such radical tactics. No one could stay with him when he imposed them. His training schedules defied all sense and reason - lap after lap after lap of the track at relentless speed, or trudging through endless knee-deep snowdrifts in army boots, at a level of intensity which even those coaches with such foresight in the 1930s and 1940s as Holmér in Sweden and Gerschler in Germany would not for one moment have imagined could have been sustained by the athletes in their charge.

Emil Zátopek's foremost achievements remain legendary:

MAJOR CHAMPIONSHIPS
(7 gold medals, 1 silver, 1 bronze) :

1946 European Championships (Oslo) - 5th 5000m.
1948 Olympic Games (Wembley) - 2nd 5000m, 1st 10,000m.
1950 European Championships (Brussels) - 1st 5000m, 1st 10,000m
1952 Olympic Games (Helsinki) - 1st 5000m, 1st 10,000m,
1st Marathon.
1954 European Championships (Berne) - 3rd 5000m, 1st 10,000m.
1956 Olympic Games (Melbourne) - 6th Marathon.

WORLD RECORDS
(20 at 10 different distances) :

5000m - 13:57.2 in 1954.
6 miles - 28:08.4 in 1953, 27:59.2 in 1954.
10,000m - 29:28.2 and 29:21.2 in 1949, 29:02.6 in 1950, 29:01.6 in 1953, 28:54.2 in 1954.
15,000m - 46:14.0 and 44:54.6 in 1951.
10 miles - 48:12.0 in 1951.
20,000m - 1:01:15.8 and 59:51.8 in 1951.
1 hour - 19,558m and 20,052m in 1951.
15 miles - 1:16:26.4 in 1952, 1:14:01.0 in 1955.

INTRODUCTION

25,000m - 1:19.11.8 in 1952, 1:16:36.4 in 1955.
30,000m - 1:35:23.8 in 1952.

The primary source of information regarding Zátopek's formative years and the greater part of his international competitive career is the biography entitled 'Zátopek The Marathon Victor', which was written by the Czech journalist, František Kozík, and published in Prague in 1954. At first glance it contains a wealth of information about Zátopek's upbringing, his early influences, his racing, his training, his thoughts, and his ideas, but it has to be recognised that this was the officially authorised version of Zátopek's life, carefully composed to satisfy the demands of the country's Communist rulers for political correctness.

Zátopek had to be presented, whether he liked it or not, as an unblemished "Hero Of the People", and as some sort of supercharged industrial worker turning out ever greater quantities of records on the track for the glorification of the Communist ideology, as if he was single-handedly manufacturing faultless gleaming tractors on a ceaseless assembly-line.

Many of Kozík's observations, expressed either in his own words or purporting to come from the mouth of Zátopek himself, smack too much of guileless propaganda to have any lasting value as a true record of achievements and aspirations. Yet such is the power of Zátopek's personality and demeanour that Kozik's occasional naive proclamations of Marxist idealism are tolerable, and to be fair to the author - hidebound as he was by the censor peering over his shoulder - he seems to have realised that he has such a good story to tell about a subject who is so obviously such a likeable individual that it needs little in the way of tawdry political justification.

Kozík simply leaves out, or glosses over, a number of matters which presumably did not fit the image or were simply too difficult to explain acceptably. For example, Zátopek was one of six children, but we are told next to nothing about the other five. Only once does the name of a coach, Josef Hron, appear in the text, and no futher reference is made as to whether he continued to have an influence on Zátopek - or if he did not, whether anyone else did.

15

ZÁ-TO-PEK! ZÁ-TO-PEK! ZÁ-TO-PEK!

Much more important than all this, though, is the irrefutable fact that Emil Zátopek was the acceptable face of Eastern Bloc sporting prowess in the latter 1940s and the early 1950s: not only a marvellous athlete, incomparable when at his best, but genuinely amiable and approachable, cheerfully dispensing advice, guidance and a helping hand to opponents even in mid-race, patiently signing autographs and posing for Box Brownie snaps with admiring fans, fellow athletes and hard-bitten Fleet Street reporters alike.

Genial, multi-lingual, seemingly tireless in his travelling and racing, Emil Zátopek - so often accompanied by his gracious wife, Dana, who shared the very same birthday and was an Olympic champion in her own right - must have caused many a spectator to wonder as the great man trundled round the track, alternately grimacing as if in his final death throes and grinning beatifically as if admiring the passing scenery, whether the Iron Curtain really did divide two cultures. Emil and Dana were faithful advocates of their nation's political creed throughout their athletics careers, and had they ever wavered they could have found open-armed sanctuary in the West whenever they wished.

Fortunately, there is an extensive and much more credible source other than Kozík from which to glean the details of Zátopek's life style. Zátopek's international career lasted from 1946 to 1956 and the latter part of it, by good fortune, has been chronicled virtually as it unfolded week after week by a remarkable journalist who was one of the first in Britain to write authoritatively and imaginatively about international athletics and who later found himself in a unique position to document the life of the greatest athlete of the era.

J. Armour Milne's detailed eye-witness accounts in the British magazine "Athletics Weekly" remain the most reliable basis for information about the great distance-runner's career, together with the regular reports given in the columns of the erudite and entertaining monthly magazine, "Athletics World", edited by the twins, Norris and Ross McWhirter, which briefly flourished during the 1950s. Otherwise, the most perceptive summary is to be found in a chapter which the eminent athletics historian (and crime novelist), Peter Lovesey, wrote in his book, "The Kings of Distance; A Study of Five Great Runners", which was

16

INTRODUCTION

published in 1968. In adding my tribute, I have also - hopefully - made selective and judicious use of the material contained within František Kozík's biography.

I am glad to say that the first edition of this book, published in 2002, proved so popular that it was sold out, and for this reissue I have made some amendments and corrections, and updated the statistics, where appropriate. Essentially, though, the contents remain very much the same as they were in their original form, but then the general consensus of opinion among those who are interested in the history of the great sport of athletics is that Emil Zátopek's place in posterity is above argument. It is more than half-a-century since he was at the peak of his physical powers, and yet I cannot imagine that anyone will think any the less of him in another 50 years, or 500, for that matter, whatever unimaginable times are being achieved by the champions of the future.

2.

THE FORMATIVE YEARS

The first "sub-four". The first "sub-15".
Zátopek is on the fringe

KOPRIVNICE IS a small town in what is now the Moravskoslez Beskydy region of Slovakia. The industrial city of Ostrava is some 40 kilometres to the North, and another 15 kilometres or so beyond that is the frontier of Southern Poland. Koprivnice is where the Tatra trucks are made, which have proved so successful in the arduous Paris-Dakar Rally, and Koprivnice was also the birthplace of another reliable performer renowned for toughness and stamina. It was there that Emil Zátopek was born on 19 September 1922.

Like most Middle European countries, what are now known separately as the Czech Republic and the Slovak Republic have a confused geography as much as a complex history. In the 10th Century the region was the Great Moravian Empire. In the 12th Century it was the Kingdom of Bohemia. In the 14th Century it was annexed to the German Empire and in the 15th Century merged with Hungary. In 1526 the Austrian Habsburg Dynasty ascended to the thrones of Bohemia and Hungary. On 28 October 1918 the Czech Republic, bringing together the Czechs and the Slovaks for the first time in eight centuries, was proclaimed.

By the terms of the Munich Pact of September 1938 Britain and France surrendered the Sudetenland border regions of Bohemia to Hitler's Nazi regime, and in March 1939 the German Army occupied the rest of the country, pronouncing the Czech lands to be the 'Protectorate of Bohemia and Moravia'. The Soviet Army ousted the Germans in May of 1945 and a year later Government was assumed by an alliance of Communists and Social Democrats. In February 1948 the Social Democrats withdrew and in July the Communists took full control and created the Czechoslovak Socialist Republic.

After the fall of the Berlin Wall free elections took place in 1990, and three years later the Czech Republic and the Slovak Republic became separate nations by mutual consent. Commonly known as Slovakia, the latter country's local name is Slovenska Republika, or Slovensko, and it is there that Emil Zátopek's birthplace is now situated.

František Kozík's biography paints an idyllic picture of the Zátopek family of six children growing up in the 1930s in a tranquil rural setting, hiking through the neighbouring meadows and fields, building wood cabins in the forests, swimming in the nearby river, tending their father's beehives. Almost inevitably, Emil was already at 10 years of age a noted runner, beating his playmates round the block, and always the one chosen by the schoolteacher to fetch and carry urgent messages. Emil's father - a carpenter in a local factory - worked hard to support the household and did not approve of frivolous sporting pastimes, according to the elaborate story told by Kozík, complete with conversational exchanges apparently recalled verbatim more than 20 years later.

The hopeful intention had been that Emil Zátopek would go on from school to teachers' training college. That did not materialise for some reason and instead he was sent off in 1937 to an apprenticeship at the Batá shoe factory at Zlín, some 90 kilometres to the South of Koprivnice, where "the conveyor belt and its capitalist masters know no mercy". The German occupation began in March of 1939 and the factory came under their control. Kozík's legend has it that Zátopek's first organised race was not until he was 18 years of age, and even then it was allegedly undertaken with great reluctance.

The date is given as 15 May 1941, and the competition is presented by Kozík as some sort of base commercial exploitation of the young employees by the factory bosses. Each Spring the workers are required to race through the streets of Zlín, which was later renamed for some years as Gottwaldov, to advertise the factory wares. Zátopek does his best to avoid being press-ganged into taking part, and that may well have been the case, though the way in which the circumstances are presented by Kozík seems to fit all too neatly into the concept of a youthful stand against the fascist establishment.

Whatever the real train of events, Zátopek finished 2nd in that factory race and was required, whether he liked it or not, to represent the Bat'á technical college students in a 1500 metres event in Brno. Again he came 2nd, and his enthusiasm had now clearly been aroused. He began some form of track training during the Spring and Summer months, and when his running partners gave up in Autumn-time he continued to train in the evening after work. In 1942 he won races at 1500 and 3000 metres and began to attract wider attention. At that time the leading Czech middle-distance and distance runners were Tomáš Šalé, who had run 1:55.0 for 800 metres and 3:57.0 for 1500 metres, and Bedrich Hošek, with 15:27.4 for 5000 metres.

With encouragement from a reputable local runner named Alí, Zátopek improved his 1500 metres time by seven seconds. In his first attempt at a 3000 metres race he finished 2nd in a respectable time of 9:12.2. Sent to Prague for the first time with the Zlín team, Zátopek helped to set a national record for the 4 x 1500 metres relay. In the 1942 national championships, again in Prague, he finished 5th in the 1500 metres in 4:13.9.

During the winter of 1942-43 Zátopek was unconsciously laying the foundations of his relentless regime of the future, running each day the eight kilometres or so to the next village and back. In 1943 he was placed 4th in the 1500 metres at the national championships but with a much improved time of 4:07.2, and it was around then - according to Kozík - that Zátopek learned something of the training principles formulated by the German coach, Toni Nett, and either of his own volition or with the encouragement of his fellow runners, Alí and Šalé, decided to concentrate on speed rather than endurance and run repeated shorter stretches.

In the Spring of 1943 he had achieved 2:00.6 for 800 metres. By the Autumn he had improved to 1:59.0. He ran 1500 metres in 4:04.6 and won the 4 x 1500 title for Zlín with a stage run in 4:02.0. In the Bohemia v Moravia match in Prague he surprised everyone, including Šalé, by winning in 4:01.0. It was the fastest time of the year by a Czech, and he also ran 15:26.6 for 5000 metres, comparing very favourably with the national record which had been held at a modest 15:12.4 by Jozef Koščák since 1934.

"People breathed again and were delighted," wrote František Kozík in his typically flowery journalistic manner. "After many years here at last was a runner who was prepared to fight. To be sure, we had a number of great runners who could give us pleasant surprises, but unfortunately they also often disappointed us. At the decisive moment their characters lacked firm unbending willpower. Now a man had appeared on the track who embodied the proverbial Slavonic tenacity that we had read of in our history books.

"He was not afraid of a struggle or of his opponents. He did not suffer from depression. He showed no respect for great names. He knew how to overcome pain and nervousness. He really knew how to master himself, and that was something unique in the history of our athletics. Yet he was only 21 years old."

These fine words do, of course, have the ring of wisdom in hindsight about them. Kozík, though a journalist by profession, apparently did not seek any views of those who were in the stadium that day when Zátopek ran his 4:01.0, and that is a pity because the meeting must have been attended by any number of coaches, journalists and fans, and among them there would certainly have been some sufficiently expert to recognise budding talent when they saw it. For once, though, the biographer's vivid imagination may well have correctly captured the mood of the moment, as it takes little effort on the part of anyone looking back to that occasion from some 60 years further on to suppose that Zátopek that day gave the more perceptive onlookers in the stand a thrill of eager anticipation for further exploits to come.

In the January of 1944 Zátopek attended a course for physical education teachers and met Josef Hron, described by Kozík as "that excellent trainer of long-distance runners". Hron invited Zátopek to a training camp for distance runners the following May, and Kozík records that Zátopek "gained a lot from the experienced trainer, and in particular was delighted to have his own training methods confirmed. From now onwards he devoted himself entirely to the interval method". He is said to have been running such sessions as 10 x 100 metres, 10 x 200 metres or 6 x 400 metres at the time.

Hron had been a reasonably successful 10,000 metres runner during the 1930s and was the fastest Czech at the distance in 1939 with a time of 33:15.1. He persuaded Zátopek to set his sights on the national 5000 metres record and clearly played a defining role in fashioning the young runner's future ambitions in the sport. Yet that, curiously, is the first and last reference which is made to Hron in Kozík's book, and the reader is left none the wiser as to whether Zátopek continued to consult Hron - or anyone else, for that matter - about training from time to time, or whether he relied entirely on his own judgment. Kozík does say that Zátopek's methods at this early stage of his career were "censured on all sides, even by his friends who cared a lot", and what does become clear in future years, despite the evidence of a multitude of successes, is that Zátopek's Herculean training schedules continued to be regarded with great suspicion by many coaches in Czechoslovakia.

Though heeding Hron's words of advice to concentrate on 5000 metres, Zátopek decided to persevere with 1500-metre running for the time being, apparently feeling he needed more training for the longer event. At the 1944 national championships he narrowly lost at 1500 to another aspiring young Czech runner, 22-year-old Václav Cevona, in 4:01.4 to 4:02.8. Later in the year, at the "Grand Prix" meeting in Prerov, 40 kilometres North of Zlín, the two of them staged a fine race and both of them broke the four-minute barrier: Cevona 3:58.9, Zátopek 3:59.5.

At a minor evening fixture on the 453-metre track at Zlín, with only 50 or so spectators in attendance, Zátopek set out to beat the national record for 3000 metres, held by Bedrich Hošek at 8:42.0, and again it seems as if it was not Zátopek's idea but someone else's. He had run 2000 metres in a time-trial faster than the national record and when news got out his club immediately set up a record attempt for him, though why it was at the longer distance was not explained. In any case, Zátopek succeeded with a time of 8:34.8, winning by 300 metres. The Prague press was sceptical of the validity of such a performance in an obscure setting by a relative unknown, but Josef Hron sent a message of support and an attempt on the 5000 metres record was set up by Zátopek's club officials for the following Saturday. He ran 14:54.9 to far exceed all the expectations of him, though

Kozík is not able to tell us anything about the details of the race or whether Zátopek received help in the pacemaking.

We can reasonably assume that this was another precocious demonstration of solo running by Zátopek because the next man, Jiri Roudný (a future European steeplechase champion), finished one and three quarter minutes behind. The following day, on the same track, Zátopek beat his mentor, Tomas Šalé, at 1000 metres after 15 defeats by him at various distances. Šalé failed to finish, and for Zátopek this was a weekend which marked a turning-point in his athletics career.

No prompting was needed for athletics enthusiasts in Czechoslovakia to realise that here was an athlete perhaps on the verge of achieving great deeds - and certainly greater deeds than those of any other Czech runner before him. Not since František Douda had broken the World record in the shot putt in 1931, and then won the bronze medal at the following year's Olympics, had Czechoslovakia had an athlete of absolutely undeniable World class. Zátopek was still some way off that level, of course.

In the straitened circumstances of wartime, the Swedes and Finns were almost unchallenged in the World rankings on the track. At 3000 metres 17 of them had run faster than 8:30.0 during 1944, but Zátopek was less than five seconds off that standard. At 5000 metres there were 20 men who had run 14:50.0 or faster - including Heino, Hägg, Reiff, Albertsson and Slijkhuis - but Zátopek now ranked 30th in the World. He was on the fringe.

Scant news had filtered through that year of such seemingly unattainable World records as Hägg's 3:43.0 for 1500 metres, Andersson's 4:01.6 for the mile, and Heino's 29:35.4 for 10,000 metres, and presumably Zátopek would have been made aware of them. Kozík's biography suggests that Zátopek regarded his 5000 metres record as being nothing special and certainly no more than the sort of time he could have expected from the level of training which he had been carrying out. Kozík does not reveal what new targets Zátopek may have set for himself, and it may be that with his country still occupied by the Germans and the imminent prospect of invasion by the Red Army - or liberation, as Kozík understandably described it - he would, like most Czechs, have had other things on his mind.

3.

INTERNATIONAL DEBUT IN 1946

Silent witnesses to a lone soldier on parade among the woodland pines

THE FINAL BATTLES between the German and Soviet armies severely disrupted life in Czechoslovakia in the winter and spring months of 1944-45, but early in 1945 Zátopek began serious training again to immediate good effect. He had been called up for military service and he won the 3000 metres at the armed forces' championships in another new national record of 8:33.4. At the national championships in Prague on 18 August he improved again at 5000 metres, with a winning time of 14:50.8 and the second man home outside 16 minutes.

His progress had been satisfying but modest. Viljo Heino, of Finland, led the World rankings for 1945 at 5000 and 10,000 metres with times of 14:17.2 and 30:02.0. Finns and Swedes had 16 of the top 20 places at 5000 metres and 17 of the top 20 at 10,000 metres. Yet, taking these two nationalities out of the reckoning, there were only four other men in the World faster than Zátopek at the shorter distance - Pujazon (France), Olesen (Denmark), Tyulenyev and Przhevalskiy (both USSR) - and Pujazon, ranked 12th in the World, was not that much faster, with a best of 14:43.4.

In October the great Arne Andersson came to Prague for what would turn out to be almost the very last races of his career before he was disqualified for breaking the rules regarding amateurism. Andersson was untroubled in winning at 2000 metres on 6 October in 5:29.6 and at 1000 metres the next day in 2:29.4. Zátopek finished behind him in both races in 5:38.6 and 2:34.6 - and according to Kozík "he returned home enriched by the experience and the friendship of such an excellent sportsman".

Zátopek was enjoying enough of Army life that he applied for and was accepted for officer training, and when he arrived at the academy in Prague he saw to his delight that there was a well-maintained running track winding round the barrack square. Though he had been warned that the demands of officer training might put an end to his athletics career, Zátopek found instead the opportunity and motivation to train more consistently. After his daytime military duties he ran on the Army track in the evening or along the nearby riverside, or under cover in the riding school during the worst of the winter months.

In the early summer of 1946 he improved the national record again at 5000 metres - and by an impressive margin, to 14:36.6. "The onlookers", wrote Kozík, "mistook his strong willpower for obstinacy. In spite of the apparent heaviness of his tread, he fought ever harder, and more and more often he came in the winner. His healthy organism was a match for all demands made upon it. Against his own nationals he was already winning by hundreds of metres".

Benefiting from the advantages of the regularity of Army life, and the opportunities he was given for taking time off to race, the pattern had been set for Zátopek's athletics future. The characteristic ungainly style, head rolling, face contorted in a grimace, arms pumping, legs pounding the track, was now a familiar sight in his homeland, though there were still plenty of critics only too ready to proclaim that his uneconomic gait and his punishing training sessions would soon put an end to him.

What they may not have known was that Zátopek was also already benefiting from expert medical and scientific support to aid his training. Dr Zdenek Hornof, from the Department of Sports Medicine at Charles University, in Prague, had first met Zátopek in 1944 and was to continue to check the athlete's health and fitness over the years that followed.

On 4 July a group of Swedish athletes competed again in Prague and Zátopek met up with one of their leading distance runners, Roland Sundin, at 3000 metres. Sundin, who the following month was to run the World's 5th fastest time of the year with 8:16.6, won the race at 8:25.6, but Zátopek was only a second or so behind in again improving the national record. In a subsequent race with Sundin at 2000 metres Zátopek again just lost but achieved another national record of 5:30.4.

In Brno on 28 July the Flying Dutchman, Willy Slijkhuis, was the invited guest for a 3000 metres race. "He ran round the track like a doe," Kozík wrote, "and the lightness of his step delighted the onlookers. Emil also gave his best. He fought every yard and kept up bravely till the straight". Both men set national records: Slijkhuis 8:15.5, Zátopek 8:21.0. "The spectators were well satisfied and honoured both runners with tremendous applause," Kozík added. "Emil, however, was not satisfied. Once again he saw how much he still had to learn."

The claim is made that Zátopek at first declined selection for the European Championships to take place in Oslo the following month because he did not think he was good enough. If, in fact, that was so, he was soon persuaded to change his mind in the interests of national honour. There were no heats for the 5000 metres and for his first race outside his home country Zátopek found himself on the starting line in the Bislett Stadium on 23 August in a dauntingly large field of 18. All of the best distance runners in the World were at the Championships.

Sydney Wooderson had set a British three miles record of 13:53.2 in beating Slijkhuis at the AAA Championships the month before. Viljo Heino had won the European title at 10,000 metres the previous day. His team-mate, Perälä, the silver-medallist, was also starting again. Reiff was running for Belgium, Nyberg and Durkfeldt for Sweden, Pujazon for France. Slijkhuis led at 3000 metres in 8:33, which represented 14:15 pace - over 20sec faster than Zátopek had ever run - and in the closing stages the tempo was even quicker, with Wooderson's famed speed taking him to victory in the second fastest time ever recorded of 14:08.6. Slijkhuis finished 30 metres behind and the rest were another 70 metres back, but Zátopek took an unexpected 5th place in 14:25.8 far ahead of Reiff.

It was a marvellous achievement by Zátopek, much faster than he had ever run before, and there were inspiring performances from several of his team-mates. Bronze medals were won by Jirí David at 200 metres, Jan Bem in the pole vault, and Miroslav Rihosek in the long jump, and by the 4 x 100 metres relay team. Václav Cevona was 4th at 1500 metres in a national record 3:53.0 behind the Scandinavians. Zátopek was by no means Czechoslovakia's only athlete of promise.

INTERNATIONAL DEBUT IN 1946

In September Zátopek was sent off to the Allied Forces' Championships at the Olympic Stadium in Berlin, and in front of a crowd of 80,000 he easily won the 5000 metres in 14:31.0 despite a long and tiring journey and almost missing the start of the race. He had now increased his training load very substantially and was daily running either 20 x 200 metres or 20 x 400 metres on the track or 12 kilometres on a woodland trail. In the Autumn of 1946 a Czech Army team travelled to Britain for the "Britannia Shield" inter-services' competition in a number of sports, including athletics, boxing, fencing and shooting, and the beneficial effects of Zátopek's methods were abundantly apparent for those who were there to see him.

A cross-country event was held on the Ascot Racecourse and Zátopek totally overwhelmed the opposition. Over a distance of not much more than six miles he won by 600 yards in a time of 34min 12sec. Reg Draper, in 3rd place for the British Army, was almost two minutes behind, and yet he had finished 10th in the International Cross-Country Championships the previous winter. Such fortunate athletics enthusiasts as might have been present that day to witness Zátopek's unheralded debut in Britain may also have noted that Etienne Gailly, of Belgium, who eventually came in 7th, was to figure in a dramatic finish to the Olympic marathon the following year.

Kozík wrote of Zátopek's training routine at the military academy at this time that he "preferred to train alone, as he could concentrate better. So he left the square and turned off into the woods. There he had discovered a cutting about 400 metres long, and so the wood paths became the silent witnesses of something that had never been seen before. A soldier running up and down till late into the night. No one forced him to do it. No one had ordered him to do it. He didn't run slowly or easily as if for fun. One could see that he forced himself to do it. He forced himself to run faster. He drew on all the strength that he still had after a day's strenuous duty. Mercilessly, he ran one lap after another. He tortured his muscles and set them ever harder tasks. He only returned home at the sounding of the last bugle call".

Fanciful as the writer's phraseology may be, it nevertheless conjurs up a graphic image in the reader's mind of the lone dedicated athlete driving himself ever onward. Like the Flying Finns, masters of distance-running for much of the century, Zátopek had set himself objectives way beyond those required merely to be the best in his own land. Unlike the Finns, Zátopek had no one to beat at home, and what admirable singleness of purpose he must have possessed on those endless dark nights! Night after night, pounding woodland paths with the aid of a pocket torch whilst his comrades-in-arms presumably lazed the hours away on their bunk beds - only Zátopek himself perhaps believing in the feasibility of faster times latent in his legs than any man had yet achieved.

Whatever second opinions he might have been seeking from time to time, there is no doubt that Zátopek already had the confidence to go it alone with his severe training, despite the opposition of many of his fellow athletes. Zátopek knew about the interval training which had been developed by Janusz Kusocinski, the great Polish runner, in the early 1930s. He was familiar with the track sesssions devised by Woldemar Gerschler which had taken Rudolf Harbig to a wondrous 800 metres World record just before the war. He had met the leading Finns and Swedes and discussed with them their preference for "speedplay" at varying pace through the forests. He would have been told that one of the Flying Finns, Taisto Mäki, had run 200 kilometres a week before breaking the World records for 5000 and 10,000 metres in the late 1930s. He had accumulated a valuable store of knowledge and felt sure that what he was doing was right.

He began the 1947 season in sensational fashion. On 8 June, after easily beating Reiff during the winter in a cross-country race in Brussels and then winning the Allied Forces' championships by a long way in Hanover, he returned to Zlín for his first major track test of the year and even though he lapped everybody in the 3000 metres race he finished in the startling time of 8:13.6. It made him the eighth fastest man ever at the distance: only Hägg, Slijkhuis, Reiff, Heino, Andersson and two other Swedes, Hellström and Kålarne, had ever run better times.

At the annual Rošický Memorial Meeting in Prague on 25 June, held in honour of a former national 800 metres champion, Evzen Rošický, who had died during the war, Zátopek met up again at 5000 metres with Evert Nyberg, the Oslo bronze-medallist from Sweden, and also in the race were two leading Finns, Väinö Koskela and Evert Heinström. Kozík gives a very detailed description of the race, complete with lap times, and the pattern of it was gloriously simple. Ignoring a stiff wind, Zátopek went straight to the front and kept hammering on until he had dropped everybody by halfway - 64.5, 67.5, 64.5, 67.5, 67.0, 69.0, 68.0 for the first seven laps, passing 2000 metres in 5:31.0 and then 3000 metres in 8:24.0. With Nyberg 40 metres down, Zátopek ran the succeeeding laps in 70.0, 69.0, 70.3, 68.7 and 72.0 but his last 200 metres was 30.2 and his final time was astonishing - 14:08.2.

This was faster than Wooderson's winning performance in the European Championships, and only Hägg's prodigious World record of 13:58.2 from 1942 remained unsurpassed. Yet even that time must now have begun to seem fallible to Zátopek because when he came to analyse his Rošický race he would have realised that he had run the first 3000 metres in 14min pace despite the difficult conditions and his preoccupation with shaking off his rivals. On a favourable day, and with only record-breaking to command his attention, surely sub-14 was possible?

Zátopek flew back to Finland with Koskela and Heinström for another 5000 metres race at the Helsinki Games on 30 June. There he found Heino, who had turned down the invitation to go to Prague, waiting for him, and the early pace was electrifying. Maybe Zátopek was already convinced that he could run much faster than he had a few days earlier. Whatever his reasoning, or that of Heino, the pair of them passed 1500 metres in 4:08, which put them on a schedule for 13:50, but competitiveness got the better of them as each in turn took the lead, and it was only in the final straight that Zátopek edged ahead to win, 14:15.2 to 14:15.4.

This was unquestionably the most important victory of Zátopek's career so far. On a Finnish track, in front of a Finnish crowd, he had beaten one of the legendary Finnish World record-holders in a contest which had demanded all of its contestants' strength and courage. No doubt the connoisseur Finnish spectators, rising to their feet in generous acclamation of Zátopek's supreme talent that evening, would have realised that here was one who was not of their own kin but who epitomised as much as any Finn had ever done the revered national characteristic of *sisu* - fighting spirit.

ZÁ-TO-PEK! ZÁ-TO-PEK! ZÁ-TO-PEK!

In Prague on 19 July Zátopek ran 14:17.2 for 5000 metres and four days later he had another wonderful record-breaking race with Willy Slijkhuis at 3000 metres, as the Dutchman won, 8:10.0 to 8:12.8. On 16 August in Prague Zátopek won the 5000 metres for Czechoslovakia against France in 14:15.0 - and the best part of a minute slower would still have sufficed to fulfil his obligation to the national team. The next man home was a 26-year-old French-Algerian who was in the process of changing his original name, Ali Mimoun-o-Kacha, to Alain Mimoun.

A day later Zátopek graduated from military school with the rank of Lieutenant, and he celebrated the following afternoon with yet another improvement at 3000 metres - to 8:08.8 in Brno. Coincidentally, this was exactly the same time as the personal bests of Slijkhuis and Reiff from the previous year and was to remain the fastest in the World throughout 1947. Another national record soon fell to Zátopek, with 5:20.6 for 2000 metres in Bratislava on 21 August.

He then went off to the World Student Games in Paris, intending to run only the 5000 metres, but he found that the race was not until the fifth day of competition so entered the 1500 metres as well. He broke his personal best of four years previously by an enormous margin in his heat with 3:55.2 and then in the final beat the favourite, Sándor Garay, of Hungary, with another huge improvement to 3:52.8. Whether or not this accidental adventure into 1500-metre running represented Zátopek's full potential, we shall never know, because he did not contest another serious race at the distance for the rest of his career. He also, of course, won the 5000 metres at the Student Games in 14:20.8.

He continued to compete prolifically and remarkably consistently throughout September and even into October. His five races at 5000 metres were all in the 14:19-to-14:23 range. He ran 8:12.2 for 3000 metres and then lost narrowly at the same distance to Reiff in Brussels on 20 September (times of 8:14.2 and 8:14.6). There was some good reason for the latter defeat because only two days before he had been at RAF Halton for the "Britannia Shield" race and had again won in majestic fashion. Already 75 yards up in the first half-mile, he completed a course of some five miles in 24min 46sec. The next man home was Lucien Theys, of Belgium, almost two minutes later - and he was to be a future International Cross-Country champion! More than once in the years to come, when the countries of the British Isles, Belgium and France met in these annual International Championships, the absence of Zátopek was to be noted upon and regretted.

The year of 1947 had truly marked the beginning of the Zátopek saga. He was the fastest man in the World at 5000 metres, and of the 12 best times of the year at the distance he had been responsible for 10. He was also fastest in the World at 3000 metres and had run six of the 10 best times there. He had even found an unexpected niche as equal 21st fastest in the World at 1500 metres. He had yet to turn his attentions to 10,000 metres, where Heino was again the leader, but the intriguing thought must have already occurred to him as he braved the wintery gloom of his woodland trail that a World record at that event only required him to maintain 14:45 pace for two successive stretches of 5000 metres.

4.

OLYMPIC YEAR OF 1948

60 x 400! What could they possibly have made of that in the Finchley clubhouse?

IN THE DECEMBER of 1947 Zátopek went on his first visit to Africa. In pouring rain he won the "*Journal d'Alger*" race through the streets of Algiers from the French 5000 metres record-holder, Jean Vernier, and some 300 others, and then had another easy victory in a 3000 metres track race on Christmas Day. During the course of the year he had run in seven foreign countries - Algeria, Belgium, Britain, Finland, France, Holland and Poland - and being the gregarious sort of person he was, with a natural charm for the people he met and a curiosity about the places he visited, he was enjoying the experience immensely.

During the winter of 1947-48 he had definitely decided, it seems, to run both the 5000 and the 10,000 metres at the Wembley Olympics, and his training had been geared accordingly. On some days he was already putting in the 60 x 400 metres sessions which were to become his hallmark, and it seems likely that he might have been experimenting with such a schedule for a year or so beforehand. Even Zátopek, with his immense powers of recovery, would have found it difficult to increase his training to that level overnight.

In Belgium in April Zátopek began his competitive preparations for the 1948 Olympics with an international 10km cross-country race over an immensely difficult course through the hills round the Ardennes town of Spa. Zátopek won, it goes without saying, in a time of 36:01.8, beating the course record by one and a half minutes, and František Kozík relates that during the bus journey back to the hotel afterwards Zátopek was bombarded with questions from his fellow-competitors about how much training he did. Teams from Belgium, Switzerland, England, Scotland and Wales had also taken part in the race, and the most inquisitive of Zátopek's interrogators were apparently the British competitors. It is an intriguing thought as to what their reaction would have been to Zátopek's replies and what the response was of their incredulous clubmates when the travellers returned home to tell the tale.

A very capable runner named John Andrews, of Finchley Harriers, was the leading Briton in Spa in 5th place in 38:20, and coincidentally he finished almost exactly the same margin behind Zátopek as he had done when Sydney Wooderson won the English National title the previous month. Andrews was running for Wales, and the English trio was Ron Hughes (Polytechnic Harriers), Fred McMinnis (Sutton Harriers) and Norman Ashcroft (Manchester AC), who were 11th, 14th and 19th respectively in Spa. McMinnis was the Northern champion that year, while Hughes had placed 11th and Ashcroft 12th in the National, and what a pity it was that Wooderson - at the end of his illustrious career - could not have been there in Belgium for a final joust with Zátopek.

On 29 May Zátopek tried himself out at 10,000 metres in a race in Budapest, and he learned a lot from the venture. He started too fast, according to Kozík, and eventually came home in a time of 30:28.4, still beating Jenö Szilágyi, who had ranked equal 11th in the World in 1947. Zátopek had also beaten out of sight the existing Czech national record, set by Jan Slezácek at 32:27.7 15 years before. More pertinently, only five men had run faster than Zátopek during 1947 - led by Heino at 30:07.4, and all of them Finns or Swedes.

Returning to his old stamping ground at Zlín on 11 June, Zátopek produced a brilliant performance with a new best of 8:07.8 for 3000 metres - and actually achieved this in the course of a 4000 metres race! Why a race should have been held at such an odd distance remains unexplained, but Zátopek treated it as a sort of competitive training session. He averaged under 2:43 for each of the first three kilometres to lead by 38 seconds and then strode through the last one in 3:06 to still win the race easily. Curiously, Kozík makes no mention of this race at all, though there is some excuse for his omission because an even more impressive feat is to come six days later. At the Strahov Stadium in Prague, Zátopek made a widely publicised debut on home ground at

10,000 metres, and although Kozík makes copious reference to the fact that Zátopek's pace judgment is better on this occasion the actual lap times are never revealed.

What Kozík, who gives the clear impression that he was among the spectators that day, does tell us is that the crowd seemed to have more understanding of what was unfolding in front of their eyes than did the officials: "We are seized with panic because according to our own reckoning even the World record might be broken … but down there in the centre no one seems to realise it. Neither the announcer nor the lap marker give Emil the slightest indication." Zátopek's time was 29:37.0, only 1.6sec slower than Heino's World record, and Kozík ends his account of the near-miss with a delightful pen-picture of the scene afterwards as Zátopek recovers his breath after winning by almost six minutes!

"The timekeepers, the officials and all of the other competitors are proud of being able to show how near they are to him. At least for a few moments they want to be able to have him entirely for themselves while they touch his tired arms."

On 22 June Zátopek produced another performance which was a highly significant pointer for the forthcoming Olympic Games. Czechoslovakia met Holland and Hungary in an international match in Prague, and Willy Slijkhuis was in the Dutch team for the 5000 metres. Zátopek led from the start and Slijkhuis followed his every move. Zátopek, as always, looked as though he was labouring. Slijkhuis was his usual elegant self, even smiling as if absolutely confident of victory. Each time Zátopek surged ahead Slijkhuiis responded with evident ease, but then with less than a kilometre to go Zátopek went away again and Slikhuis could not close the gap. He stepped off the track soon afterwards and Zátopek went on to win in 14:10.0, which was to be the fastest time in the World for the year.

Gaston Reiff had run 5000 metres in 14:14.2 on 16 June, and the response to Zátopek's times from the Scandinavians in July was also a positive one. Erik Ahldén, of Sweden, ran 14:13.2 for 5000 metres and Salomon Könönen, of Finland, won a 10,000 metres in Helsinki in 30:10.8. Nobody, not even Nurmi, had taken the gold medals at both the 5000 metres and the 10,000 metres at the same Olympic Games since

Hannes Kolehmainen had done so in 1912. The prospects of Zátopek emulating Kolehmainen looked good, but Reiff and Slijkhuis would concentrate all their efforts on the 5000 and Heino all his on the 10,000.

The 10,000 metres took place on Friday 30 July, which was the opening day of athletics at Wembley Stadium. There were 27 starters and the principals among them, with their best times, were as follows :

Heino (Finland) 29:35.4, Zátopek (Czechoslovakia) 29:37.0, Könönen (Finland) 30:10.8, Heinström (Finland) 30:11.0, Stokken (Norway) 30:24.4, Albertsson (Sweden) 30:26.4, Dennolf (Sweden) 30:50.0, Paris (France) 31:02.0, Miranda (Spain) 31:02.6, Ben Said Abdallah (France) 31:02.8, Bralo (Argentina) 31:09.0, Guinez (Argentina) 31:09.8, Everaert (Belgium) 31:12.0, Mimoun (France) 31:21.0, Kjersem (Norway) 31:30.2, Lataster (Belgium) 31:30.8, Wilt (USA) 31:33.4.

It obviously gave all the promise of being a two-man race. Heino went straight into the lead from Albertsson and Heinström and the first kilometre was covered in 2:55.6, which was well inside World-record pace. At 2000 metres, reached in 5:52.0, it was still 29:20 pace. At 3000 metres (8:51.0) Zátopek was back in the melee in 17th place, but within two laps he had moved up to 4th and during the next kilometre he went into the lead. Heino was in front again at halfway (14:57.0), but the tempo had steadily dropped in the stiflingly hot conditions - 2:56, 2:56, 2:59, 3:01, 3:05 for successive kilometres - and when Zátopek ran 3:03 for the next kilometre it was too much for Heino, who dropped out after 16 laps. The French-Algerian, Alain Mimoun, was the only man in the first six to improve on his previous best as Zátopek won by the best part of a lap. The result was as follows:

1 Zátopek (Czechoslovakia) 29:59.6 (Olympic record), 2 Mimoun (France) 30:47.4, 3 Albertsson (Sweden) 30:53.6, 4 Stokken (Norway) 30:58.6, 5 Dennolf (Sweden) 31:05.0, 6 Abdallah Ben Said (France) 31:07.8, 7 Cox (GB) 31:08.0, 8 Peters (GB) 31:16.0, 9 Könönen (Finland), 10 O'Toole (USA), 11 Wilt (USA).

ZÁ-TO-PEK! ZÁ-TO-PEK! ZÁ-TO-PEK!

In the confusion of so many runners being lapped the officials failed to record any times beyond 8th place or register any positions beyond 11th, except that the Frenchman, Paris, was 23rd and last. Heinström, as well as Heino, was a non-finisher.

The heats of the 5000 metres took place the next day and Zátopek, Albertsson and Stokken were among the 12 qualifiers for the final on 2 August. Mimoun, who had lost 2kg in weight during the 10,000 metres, was eliminated. Zátopek, totally unnecessarily, chased the Swede, Ahldén, home when he could have run half-a-minute slower and still qualified. The finalists, and their best times, were the following:

Zátopek (Czechoslovakia) 14:08.2, Ahldén (Sweden) 14:13.2, Slijkhuis (Holland) 14:14.0, Reiff (Belgium) 14:14.2, Albertsson (Sweden) 14:20.2, Nyberg (Sweden) 14:23.2, Perälä (Finland) 14:25.6, Koskela (Finland) 14:28.0, Stokken (Norway) 14:31.0, Mäkelä (Finland) 14:45.8, Stone (USA) 14:49.1, van de Wattyne (Belgium) 14:49.2.

The weather was in complete contrast to the 10,000 metres. It was raining and cool. The Wembley cinders were unhelpfully yielding. Zátopek's tactics were also very different. He led from the start but merely at a testing pace rather than a destructive one. The time at 2000 metres was 5:38.0, which was 14:05 schedule. The next kilometre was much slower at 2:55.0 and when Reiff moved ahead Zátopek seemed to have no answer. The fourth kilometre took 2:52.0 and Reiff was on his own, leading Slijkhuis by 30 metres and Zátopek by twice that.

The race seemed over, and it was not until the last lap that Zátopek, from 50 metres down, began to make any impression. His last 200 metres was phenomenal: gaining on Reiff with every stride to the frenzied excitement of the crowd he closed to within a yard or so of the leader. Unfortunately for the 10,000 metres champion, the finishing line intervened and Reiff hung on to win. The familiar photograph of the finish shows Reiff, arms spread as if in despair, looking agonisingly over his shoulder at the fearsome spectacle of the red-vested pursuer bearing down on him. Reiff has the look of the vanquished; Zátopek that of the victor, but Reiff had the gold, and deservedly so, for his brave mid-race effort, and the silver had to suffice for Zátopek. The full result, again with the officials unable to supply complete timings, was as follows:

1 Reiff (Belgium) 14:17.6, 2 Zátopek (Czechoslovakia) 14:17.8, 3 Slijkhuis (Holland) 14:26.8, 4 Ahldén (Sweden) 14:28.6, 5 Albertsson (Sweden) 14:39.0, 6 Stone (USA) 14:39.4, 7 Koskela (Finland) 14:41.0, 8 Mäkelä (Finland) 14:43.0, 9 van de Wattyne (Belgium), 10 Stokken (Norway), 11 Perälä (Finland). Did not finish: Nyberg (Sweden).

It has to be said that Zátopek had not run the most sensible of races. There was no reason for him to bear the brunt of the weather and lead his two main rivals, neither of whom had taken part in the 10,000 metres. If he felt he had to lead, then he should have done so at a faster pace, or he should have varied the pace. When Reiff attacked at 3500 metres Zátopek should have hung on to him grimly at whatever cost, in the knowledge that the Belgian was known to be vulnerable when under pressure. Maybe that injudicious sparring with Ahldén in the heats had weakened Zátopek.

All of this, of course, is easy to say. The race simply served to show that Zátopek was no automaton, and that he could be beaten if someone had the resolution to do so. Reiff was one of the finest runners of his generation and was to set marvellous new World records of 5:07.0 for 2000 metres a month later and 7:58.8 for 3000 metres the following year. Against the clock, and at these intermediate distances, he was in his element. Usually in the major Championships he failed to match expectations, but he took his chance at Wembley, and though Zátopek was to run many more 5000 metres races of outstanding quality, including a World record, he probably already realised that eventually he would not be able to hold his own at that distance against runners like Reiff, who possessed so much greater speed. Reiff had already run 1500 metres in 3:48.4 and was to improve to 3:45.8 in 1949.

The Czech athletes, under their new Communist Party rulers, had yet to start to benefit from State aid, but Cevona was 4th in the 1500 metres and a 25-year-old ex-handball player, Dana Ingrová, had placed an encouraging 7th in the women's javelin.

ZÁ-TO-PEK! ZÁ-TO-PEK! ZÁ-TO-PEK!

On a mini-tour after the Games Zátopek won at 3000 metres in Brussels on 13 August (8:18.0) but was well beaten into 3rd place by Ahldén and Slijkhuis in Amsterdam two days later: respective times of 8:09.6, 8:10.2 and 8:16.0. He won races at 5000 metres (14:21.4) in Prague on 18 August and at 3000 metres (8:16.2) in Brno two days afterwards. Gaston Reiff courageously agreed to a return match with Zátopek at 5000 metres on 12 September and won again, by 14:19.0 to 14:21.2. It was back in Brussels at the end of the month that Reiff ran his 2000 metres World record, beating the time set by Hägg six years earlier by a margin of 2.4sec. Reiff's record, in turn, lasted six years.

On 26 September Zátopek struggled through the second half of a 10,000 metres in Bucharest, with his hip giving him problems, to finish in 30:03.6, but he was still required to turn out for the Czechoslovak national team in their match against Italy at the beginning of October, and despite his injury he won both his races in 14:30.2 and 30:09.8.

Even then his season was not yet over, and he returned to Prague where at a floodlit evening meeting - very rare for those days - he convincingly beat the Swede, Ahldén, at 5000 metres in 14:16.8. Zátopek had run seven of the 12 fastest times in the World during the year at that distance, and four of the six best times at 10,000 metres. Viljo Heino had regained some credibility with a 30:03.2 for 10,000 in Oslo on 23 September, but at 34 it might seem as if his days were over. Zátopek, dedicated student of the sport that he was, would not have complacently written him off yet. He had too much respect for the great tradition of the Flying Finns.

On 24 October 1948 Emil was married to Dana Ingrová, the ex-handball player. Their compatibility was predestined. Dana's birthday was exactly the same as her husband's. The ceremony, of course, had to be arranged around Zátopek's athletics commitments, and that was something to which the new Mrs Zátopek was going to have to get accustomed. As it happens, she had been born six hours earlier than her new husband, and she was to remain a lady of indomitable spirit who gave Emil unstinted support on and off the track whilst also forging an outstanding athletics career of her own.

38

5.

THE FIRST WORLD RECORD IN 1949

Hurtling through the cool twilight as though he was possessed

EMIL ZÁTOPEK began the 1949 season in impressive fashion. After an easy run-out of 14:23.6 in Prague on 4 May he was in Warsaw five days later for another 5000 metres race and produced a time of 14:10.2. Only Zátopek himself and Sydney Wooderson had ever run faster in postwar years.

Zátopek then went to Ostrava, not far from where he was born, to run in the Czech Army championships, and it may be that his original intention was simply to fulfil a military obligation. Kozík certainly says that there was no thought of record-breaking in mind at the start of the 10,000 metres on the evening of 11 June, but Zátopek must have realised early on in the race that great things were possible. Already at 2km he was ahead of the schedule which had taken Heino to his 29:35.4 five years previously. At 3km Zátopek went through in 8:43.0, and he was over nine seconds faster than Heino. At 7km Zátopek's advantage was 12.8sec. He lost some ground in the last kilometre but at the finish he was still well inside the World record - 29:28.2. The respective times of Heino and Zátopek for each kilometre "split" and progressively had been as follows:

Heino 29:35.4, Helsinki, 25 August 1944

2:56.0	2:56.4	3:00.0	2:59.0	2:58.0	3:00.0	3:00.4	2:56.0	2:58.8	2:50.8
	5:52.4	8:52.4	11:51.4	14:49.4	17:49.4	20:49.8	23:45.8	26:44.6	29:35.4

ZÁ-TO-PEK! ZÁ-TO-PEK! ZÁ-TO-PEK!

Zátopek 29:28.2, Ostrava, 11 June 1949

2:54.5 2:54.5 2:54.0 2:57.7 2:58.8 2:59.5 2:58.0 3:00.0 2:59.0 2:52.2
5:49.0 8:43.0 11:40.7 14:39.5 17:39.0 20:37.0 23:37.0 26:36.0 29:28.2

Only Zátopek would then have had the temerity to return to Ostrava a week later for another 10,000 metres in an international match against Rumania. Whether he thought he could improve further, or it was just a sense of duty that took him there, he ran 29:49.6 and paid a price for it because when he raced at 5000 metres in Stockholm on 15 June he suffered a leg muscle injury, though still winning in 14:14.4. A month's treatment and recovery did him good and he went off to Helsinki to take on the formidable task of running for Czechoslovakia against Finland at 10,000 metres and 5,000 metres on successive days, 12-13 July.

Heino and Könönen were the Finnish pair on the first day, and the latter set off at a tremendous speed, but Zátopek paid him not much heed, ran his own race, and in the end won quite comfortably in 29:58.4. The next day Koskela and Mäkelä were Finland's representatives, and after Mäkelä had tried the same tactics early on Koskela forced the pace in the latter stages, but Zátopek dug deep into his reserves and just got by to win again in 14:20.0 to Koskela's 14:20.8. Cevona took the 1500 metres in 3:50.4 and Finland won the match by only seven points. Zátopek beat Koskela in two more desperately close races immediately afterwards: both running 14:13.2 for 5000 metres in Turku on 15 July, and Zátopek winning 8:19.2 to 8:19.4 over 3000 metres in Pori two days later.

There were still more international-match commitments to be fulfilled. This, after all, was the cornerstone of athletics competition in those days. There were very few open meetings and no lucrative Grand Prix series. Athletics was ostensibly an amateur sport, and most countries abided by the rules, but for state-aided competitors from Eastern European countries there were less problems to be faced regarding the mere matter of earning a living, and success in a nation-to-nation encounter was seen by their political masters as being the perfect demonstration of a superior way of life.

In Moscow on 25 July for the first USSR v Czechoslovakia encounter Zátopek won the 5000 metres in 14:29.0 from Vladimir Kazantsev, who set a national record of 14:30.0, and three days later Zátopek beat Kazantsev again in a 10,000 metres. In Budapest on 29-30 August Zátopek won against Hungary and Italy at 5000 metres and again at 10,000 metres in 30:00.4, with his nearest rival finishing in 31:41.0. Against Rumania in Bucharest on 10-11 September he won another double in 14:24.0 and 30:01.2, and that really ought to have brought his season to a close. He had run 5000 metres in 14:24.0 or better on six occasions during the year, and only four other men had recorded that sort of level of performance - Koskela, Mäkelä, Jacques Vernier (France) and Bertil Albertsson (Sweden). Zátopek had run 22 races at 5000 and 10,000 metres and had won them all.

He must surely have been taken aback, though, when he heard that Heino, whom he had beaten so easily in July, had retrieved his World record at Kouvola on 1 September with a time of 29:27.2. Zátopek had a high regard for Heino, and even many years later when he was interviewed just before his 70th birthday by the Slovak journalist, Ladislav Krnac, he paid the Finn warm tribute: "Heino was a fighter and a very ambitious man. He lost his best years of running because of World War II, and otherwise he would have been under 29 minutes. After races he used to be more friendly than most of my other rivals of those days, and we have met several times more since then, but one race he never talked about was the 1948 Olympic 10,000 metres, where he failed to finish. He was too proud for that".

Kozík says that Zátopek's initial response to Heino's achievement was merely that he would try and set a new record some time the following year, but "everybody who knew him felt the inner disquiet beneath his apparent indifference". In Ostrava on 17 September Zátopek ran 29:38.2, and while there is no suggestion that this was a record attempt it may well have been a deliberate test to assess his fitness after constant travelling had forced him to miss a lot of training.

He soon made up for it. Asked if he would like a record attempt arranged at the Ostrava track where he had already raced the distance on three occasions during the year, including his World record in June, he replied that he would need three weeks of hard training to be ready. So a provisional date was set for 20 October.

His first day of preparations involved 5 x 200 metres, 20 x 400 metres and 5 x 200 metres, with the 200-metres stretches as fast as he could and the 400-metre stretches at 10,000 metres pace. From the second day to the 15th day he ran 5 x 200, 30 x 400, 5 x 200 each day. In the third week he repeated the first day's session but rested on two of the days because of another leg strain. On the 20th day he ran 5 x 200, 10 x 400, 5 x 200. He also contrived to fit in a couple of races at 5000 and 10,000 metres to avoid any accusations of taking things easy!

It hardly seemed an ideal situation, but Kozík says that "he was once more in his customary record-breaking mood. In this state Emil could endure incredibly hard training. At the same time he anxiously watched his body. On the track he gave it no rest. Remorselessly, he forced it to endure the utmost exertion". Worries about the leg problems he had suffered in June meant that it was not until two days beforehand that it was finally decided to go ahead with the attack on Saturday 22 October. Laps in 70sec apiece would produce an aggregate of 29:10.0, and he eventually decided to aim for alternate lap times of 70 and 71 with a final target of 29:23.0.

Even at such short notice 20,000 people crowded into the Vitkovice Stadium for the race to begin at 4.15 in the afternoon, and a number of Zátopek's ATK (Army Sports Club) colleagues - Šourek, Klominek, Novák, Augustin, Kolár - lined up with him, though there was never any serious possibility of any of them aiding in the pacemaking. In any case, there was no need for them to do anything but make up the numbers because Zátopek knew that it was all up to him.

His judgment was faultless. By 3000m he was 2.8sec up on Heino. At 5000 metres (14:38.0) he was comfortably inside his schedule and six seconds up on Heino. For the rest of the way he kept the advantage at between six and eight seconds. Kozík, with his colourful journalese, takes up the story on the last lap:

Emil hurtles through the cool twilight as though possessed, full of energy and mad with determination. Now it is no longer just a question of the willpower of the runner down there. Now it is our common willpower which unites in a mighty outpouring that steels Emil's heart and muscles, that drives him on to the goal. Three hundred metres from the post he flings in all the energy and strength that has somehow lain stored away. Our shouts carry him forward. His running becomes a victorious careering dash. Only fifty metres separate him from the tape, and then the exhausted athlete, who seems to be running almost subconsciously, raises his head to the stands and smilingly waves to us. He is quite sure of the record now. He breaks the tape and the pistol shots announce that the World record is ours again. 29 minutes 21.2 seconds! Emil Zátopek had won back the World record for his country!

Heino 29:27.2, Kouvola, 1 September 1949

2:53.2	2:53.8	3:00.8	2:56.2	3:00.0	2:59.8	2:56.4	2:59.8	2:57.4	2:49.8
	5:47.0	8:47.8	11:44.0	14:44.0	17:43.8	20:40.2	23:40.0	26:37.4	29:27.2

Zátopek 29:21.2, Ostrava, 22 October 1949

2:55.0	2:55.9	2:54.1	2:57.0	2:56.0	2:58.0	2:57.5	2:59.5	2:57.5	2:50.7
	5:50.9	8:45.0	11:42.0	14:38.0	17:36.0	20:33.5	23:33.0	26:30.5	29:21.2

In the October issue of the UK monthly magazine, "Athletics", there appeared an article entitled "Training for the Distances ... The Zátopek Way". It had first been published in the German weekly, "*Leichtathletik*", and had been written by a coach in Prague, Klement Kerssenbrock, and translated by Jim Alford, who was then the National Coach for Wales and knew a fair bit about running from first-hand experience, having been the British Empire Games mile champion in 1938.

Kerssenbrock did not make any claims to having had a hand in Zátopek's training, and in fact gives much more credit for that to Josef Hron than Kozik ever did. Kerssenbrock states firmly that "Zátopek had the good fortune to come into the hands of our best long-distance specialist, Hron, who carefully guided his path from an 800 metres runner to a champion at the long distances. Today Zátopek has naturally profited from his own experience, but he still pays tribute to his mentor.."

Kerssenbrock continued: "Those who look for something sensational in Zátopek's training will be disappointed, for it is extremely simple. Despite much well-meant advice to fashion his training according to the Swedish or Finnish principles, or after the manner of some great runner or other, Zátopek trains as best suits himself. The basic principle of his work lies in daily training - in wind and rain, blizzard or heat wave, throughout the whole year without interruption. If his work necessitates his being in the countryside, he runs in the forest, the fields, or on the road. If he is staying in a town, he trains on the track, no matter what time of the year it is. In bad weather he wears Army boots; otherwise, according to the terrain, rubber shoes or running shoes with short spikes.

"His own special training is a combination of 'Interval' (this means running specific stretches at a fast pace with intervals of slow running interspersed) and 'Variation of Speed' running. Usually, in training he runs 200 metres five times, and then 400 metres 20 (!) times, and then once again 200 metres five times. The above distances are not, however, separate runs but spurts which are joined together by about 200 metres of light running. The speed and number of these fast sectors of running are governed by the part of the season in which he is training, his condition at the time, the weather and competitions etc.

"In winter the distances are run at a slower pace and the 'rest periods' are shaded off imperceptibly. As the season advances, the speed is increased. During the slower sectors the breathing is brought back again to something like the normal. If speed is lacking, more 200 metres sectors are included, while if endurance is thought to be more needed the 400 metres sectors are increased. Thus the number may increase up to 30 or 40.

"I saw Zátopek in training run as many as 60 of these fast 400 metres sectors! That is a tremendous amount of work when you calculate that he carried out 24km (about 15 miles) of fast running, and in all with the slower 'recovery' sectors included he covered 36km (about 22 miles). This, of course, did not happen at every training session, but two or three times a month the training was as severe as this, and then tapered off a little. Last year, when he was concentrating on the longer distance, he ran the 400 metres 60 times for 10 days at a stretch.

"This programme already includes the warming up, for Zátopek acknowledges no separate 'limbering up'. The first runs are always taken somewhat easier, then gradually speeded up, and then again tapered off towards the end of the training session. He carries out no gymnastic exercises on principle. To him the run was everything. So, like every true runner, Zátopek has an uncommonly fine instinct with which he senses the correct proportion, speed and form of his individual training. He always knows exactly when he lacks speed or stamina. He always has the best knowledge of his own condition. He never has times called out to him during his training. He often trains this way right up to the day of a race. Only when he feels a little tired does he rest for one or two days before serious competition.

"He always takes his races very seriously. His scheme of training allows him to break down the opposition by innumerable spurts interspersed during the race, and still to add to that an amazing finish. He has accustomed himself always to increase the speed still more at the moment when fatigue appears to be overcoming him. The title 'running machine' therefore does not quite fit him. For there is no trace of machine-like uniformity in his running, even if the many small changes in speed are not visible to the spectators. His opponents can certainly tell you about them!"

ALL-TIME BEST PERFORMANCES AT 5000 METRES

At the end of 1949:

13:58.2 Gunder Hägg (Sweden)	(1)	Gothenburg (WR)	20.09.42
14:08.2 Emil Zátopek (Czech)	(1)	Prague	25.06.47
14:08.6 Sydney Wooderson (GB)	(1)	Oslo (ECh)	23.08.46
14:08.8 Taisto Mäki (Finland)	(1)	Helsinki (WR)	16.06.39
14:09.6 Viljo Heino (Finland)	(1)	Gothenburg	17.09.44
14:10.0 Zátopek	(1)	Prague	22.06.48
14:10.2 Zátopek	(1)	Warsaw	09.05.49
14:11.4 Heino	(1)	Helsinki	20.06.44
14:13.2 Erik Ahldén (Sweden)	(1)	Gävle	21.07.48
14:13.2 Zátopek	(1)	Turku	15.07.49
14:13.2 Väinö Koskela (Finland)	(2)	Turku	15.07.49
14:14.0 Willy Slijkhuis (Holland)	(2)	Oslo (ECh)	23.08.46
14:14.2 Gaston Reiff (Belgium)	(1)	Brussels	16.06.48
14:14.4 Zátopek	(1)	Stockholm	15.06.49
14:15.0 Zátopek	(1)	Prague	16.08.47
14:15.2 Zátopek	(1)	Helsinki	30.06.47
14:15.4 Heino	(2)	Helsinki	30.06.47
14:15.8 Bror Hellström (Sweden)	(1)	Stockholm	28.09.41
14:16.2 Kauko Pekuri (Finland)	(2)	Helsinki	16.06.39
14:16.8 Zátopek	(1)	Prague	13.10.48

ZÁ-TO-PEK! ZÁ-TO-PEK! ZÁ-TO-PEK!

WR - World record. ECh - European Championships. Total of 20 performances at sub-14:17.0: Zátopek 8; Heino 3; Hägg, Wooderson, Mäki, Ahldén, Koskela, Slijkhuis, Reiff, Hellström, Pekuri 1 each. Note: Hägg's second best performance was 14:24.4 in 1944.

N.B. Finishing position in race in brackets.

ALL-TIME BEST PERFORMANCES AT 10,000 METRES

At the end of 1949:

29:21.2 Emil Zátopek (Czech)	(1)	Ostrava (WR)	22.10.49
29:27.2 Viljo Heino (Finland)	(1)	Kouvola (WR)	01.09.49
29:28.2 Zátopek	(1)	Ostrava (WR)	11.06.49
29:35.4 Heino	(1)	Helsinki (WR)	25.08.44
29:35.8 Heino	(1)	Karhula	21.08.49
29:37.0 Zátopek	(1)	Prague	17.06.48
29:38.2 Zátopek	(1)	Ostrava	17.09.49
29:49.6 Zátopek	(1)	Ostrava	18.06.49
29:52.0 Heino	(1)	Oslo (ECh)	22.08.46
29:52.6 Taisto Mäki (Finland)	(1)	Helsinki (WR)	17.09.39
29:53.0 Alain Mimoun (France)	(1)	Oslo	22.09.49
29:55.6 Heino	(1)	Karhula	22.09.46
29:56.2 Heino	(1)	Helsinki	03.08.44
29:58.0 Martin Stokken (Norway)	(2)	Oslo	22.09.49
29:58.4 Zátopek	(1)	Helsinki	12.07.49
29:59.6 Zátopek	(1)	London (OG)	30.07.48
29:59.6 Stokken	(1)	Stockholm	10.09.49
30:00.4 Zátopek	(1)	Budapest	30.08.49
30:01.2 Zátopek	(1)	Bucharest	11.09.49
30:02.0 Heino	(1)	Helsinki	02.09.45

OG - Olympic Games. Total of 20 performances at 30:02.0 or better: Zátopek 9; Heino 7; Stokken 2; Mäki, Mimoun 1 each.

6.

EUROPEAN CHAMPIONSHIPS IN 1950

Separate races. One for Zátopek;
the other for those who struggled for 2nd

DESPITE A LEGACY going back to Alfred Shrubb at the turn of the century, runners from Great Britain had made surprisingly little impact at 5000 and 10,000 metres on the track until Sydney Wooderson came along at the end of a war-disrupted career and won the European title at 5000 metres in the second fastest time ever recorded. It was the only race that Wooderson ran at the distance and it was a final fling, because he retired from track competition after that.

There was never any suggestion that Wooderson, at 33, would have continued into the Olympic year of 1948 and taken on Reiff, Slijhuis and Zátopek at Wembley. He now had a living to earn in the legal profession, and athletics for him became a recreational pastime which nevertheless enabled him to win the 1948 National cross-country championship over a hilly nine-mile course and to still turn out many years later for his lifelong club, Blackheath Harriers, at the age of 54 to run a mile relay stage in celebration of their centenary. Unlike Zátopek, who had promotions and honours lavished upon him from the earliest days of his international successes, Wooderson had to wait for more than 60 years to be officially recognised by his country.

Wooderson was unquestionably one of the greatest "all-round" runners of his generation - or, for that matter, any generation which followed. He broke the World records for 800 metres, 880 yards and the mile. He was European champion at 1500 metres before the war and at

5000 metres eight years later. He ran 440 yards in 49.3sec. He ran 10 miles cross-country in 55min 11sec. It is not at all unreasonable to assume that had he been able to continue racing at the highest level after his 14:08.6 for 5000 metres in 1946 he would have, at the very least, threatened Gunder Hägg's World record of 13:58.2 from 1942... but then Hägg himself could surely have run very much faster.

Of the 44 races which Hägg contested during his halcyon years of 1941-42 only two were at three miles or 5000 metres - and in each instance he broke the World record. It needs little imagination to conjecture that a man who had set World records of 3:43.0 for 1500 metres, 4:01.4 for the mile, 5:11.8 for 2000 metres, 8:01.2 for 3000 metres and 8:42.8 for two miles was perfectly capable of running 13:50 or better at 5000 metres. The International Amateur Athletic Federation Scoring Tables, which had been devised to enable comparisons to be made between different events, gave only limited value even to Zátopek's new 10,000 metres record. Fortune Gordien's discus throw of 56.97metres in 1949 rated highest with 1,296 points. Cornelius Warmerdam's 4.77m pole vault from 1942 was next at 1,292pts. Jim Fuchs's shot putt of 17.79m, also from the previous year, was 3rd with 1,252pts. Zátopek's 29:21.2 for 10,000 metres was a long way down the list - 12th at 1,155pts.

All of the performances by Hägg at distances up to 3000 metres were way beyond Zátopek's level of achievement at the end of the 1940s and would remain so throughout his career. Hägg had also run 800 metres in 1:52.8, compared with Zátopek's best of 1:59.0. Zátopek simply seemed not to have any semblance of basic speed remotely approaching that of Hägg, and even Nurmi back in the 1920s had run a much faster 800 metres (1:56.3) than had Zátopek. The Finns and the Swedes trained hard. Wooderson less so. Zátopek had realised early on that he had to train at a far more intense level than anyone had ever done to make up for what he lacked in natural ability.

In the early months of 1950 the British reaction to the news filtering through of Zátopek's training methods was one of bemusement. Jimmy Green, editor of "Athletics Weekly" magazine and himself a distance runner of county class, wrote in the issue for 4 March: "I have yet to hear of any athlete who can manage anything approaching the Czech's programme. Frankly, I do not think we have a runner in this country who could do so, no matter how long he might spend in working up to it".

The subject came up again in the issue for 25 March and Green reflected what must have been a spreading realisation among the more thoughtful of British club runners that Zátopek's way was the way forward, but how was anyone in Britain in 1950 going to find the time to carry out such schedules, even if they had the physique and the single-mindedness to do so? There was no sponsorship, no trust funds, no sports scholarships, no extravagantly indulgent employers to accommodate the ambitions of distance runners in those days, and the only financial inducements were the risky under-the-counter payments which had led to the disqualification of Hägg and Andersson in Sweden.

Green, brought up in the belief that a couple of runs during the week and a race on Saturday was quite enough for anybody, wrote in a tone of admonishment: "Zátopek is, of course, a law unto himself when it comes to training, and no athlete would be wise to emulate his colossal amount of severe work. It combines the fast/slow/fast/slow work with punishing severity. The quantity and severity of his training and racing are such that it was fully anticipated he would not last for more than a couple of years at the same rate, but the Czech is still running and breaking records".

When Peter Lovesey, the celebrated novelist and athletics historian, came to write his widely-lauded book, "The Kings of Distance: A Study of Five Great Runners", in 1968 he chose for his subjects Deerfoot, George, Shrubb, Nurmi and Zátopek. Had the author come to compose another edition 30 years later he might have added Kuts, Elliott, Clarke, Snell and Gebrselassie, and even perhaps others, but his original choices still stand as the great innovators in their events. Deerfoot, the exotic Red Indian professional "pedestrian" who took on all-comers in challenge matches in the 1860s and ran 10 miles in 51min 26sec. Walter George, who at the age of 19 announced his intention of running a mile in 4min 12sec and all but did so eight years later in 1886. Alfred Shrubb, who broke the half-hour for six miles on a winter's day in Glasgow in 1904. Nurmi, the Flying Finn, the Silent Executioner of the Stopwatch, who won Olympic gold medals galore and achieved World records for 1500 metres and 5000 metres within the hour one evening in 1924. And Zátopek.

ZÁ-TO-PEK! ZÁ-TO-PEK! ZÁ-TO-PEK!

"We were totally unprepared for Zátopek," Lovesey wrote. "In 1948 we were still spellbound by that fantastic figure, Nurmi. The sovereignty of Finnish distance running was everywhere revered. Nurmi's records had vanished, but they had fallen to his countrymen, who studied his methods, trained with equal resolution, and aped his style".

In the early months of 1950 little was heard of Zátopek, but there could be no doubt that he was preparing more strenuously than ever before for the new season, with the European Championships in Brussels as the main objective. As in Oslo four years previously, the best distance runners in the World would be brought together there. Still no Central Africans, no Asians, no Americans, no Australians or New Zealanders had emerged to offer any serious post war challenge to Europe.

Zátopek and his wife, Dana, had spent a month at Sochi, on the Black Sea, at a training camp for Soviet athletes. It was heard that Zátopek was running more than 25km a day of 400-metre efforts, and that for two weeks in June he ran 32km in this way - 80 x 400 metres! He was reported as saying that he would attack his 5000 metres best of 14:08.2 and that he had set himself a target of 29:15 for 10,000 metres as a prelude in early August to the European Championships. After some easy run-outs in May, he eventually appeared on the track on 10 June in Prague, running 14:17.2 for 5000 metres, and even during July his winning performances were relatively low-key: 14:31.0 in the match against Poland on 2 July, 29:54.2 and 14:28.6 in Bratislava the next weekend, 14:22.6 in Brno on 14 July. His training programme, aimed exclusively at a new World record and then winning in Brussels, was taking all precedence.

The intention had been that Zátopek would go for the 10,000 metres record at the Army championships on the Ostrava track which he knew so well, but then politics intervened. For no apparent good reason - other than to serve the propaganda purposes of his country's rulers - Zátopek was sent off to Finland in response to an invitation from the workers' trade union, TUL. There would be no opposition worthy of the name, but he would run a 5000 metres in Helsinki on 2 August and a 10,000 metres in Turku two days later. Presumably, Zátopek adjusted to the hurried new arrangements with good grace, as a serving Army officer and a loyal supporter of the regime. Maybe, the thought of shifting his record attempts to the ancestral home of distance-running, even at the risk of disappointing his homeland supporters, appealed to his impish sense of humour.

In Helsinki he ran splendidly: 14:06.2 for 5000 metres; his fastest time by two seconds, and the nearest approach yet to Hägg's ageing record. Zátopek completed the first kilometre in 2:48.0 and at 3000 metres in 8:27.0 a final time of something very close to 14 minutes or even to Hägg's record still seemed feasible, but the fourth kilometre - either through sheer fatigue or by design - took 2:53.0. The next man home ran 14:43.0.

In Turku - which, by such sweet irony, happened to be Paavo Nurmi's birthplace - Zátopek ran magnificently: a new World record for 10,000 metres of 29:02.6 which far exceeded everyone's expectations, except maybe his own private musing. He did not begin the race with any obvious flourish, running the first kilometre in 2:58, but he passed halfway in 14:37.0 and then ran the second part of the race in 14:25.6. To put that astounding achievement into its proper perspective of the era, it should be pointed out that the previous year only five other men in the World had achieved better than 14:25.6 - and they, of course, had been running merely in 5000 metres races!

Zátopek 29:02.6, Turku, 4 August 1950

2:58.0   2:53.8   2:54.2   2:55.5   2:55.5   2:54.0   2:53.0   2:56.0   2:55.0   2:47.6
          5:51.8   8:46.0   11:41.5 14:37.0 17:31.0 20:24.0 23:20.0 26:15.0 29:02.6

This was a performance of the utmost significance. Zátopek had sustained a tempo of running far beyond the capabilities of any of his illustrious predecessors. He was in front and on his own after two laps, though that would have been a familiar experience for him, and he finished the best part of 2½ laps ahead of the next man. He had run the sixth and seventh kilometres together 10 seconds faster than anyone else had ever done in a 10,000 metres race. Had there been a timekeeper at six miles he would have had another World record because he certainly passed that mark in about 28:05, far inside Heino's offical 28:30.8.

ZÁ-TO-PEK! ZÁ-TO-PEK! ZÁ-TO-PEK!

Most significantly of all, he had broken the record by a wider margin than anyone had managed since Paavo Nurmi, 29 years earlier in 1921. So he had taken the event towards a new level, with a time of under 29 minutes now well within reach. In Tampere three days later he was required to run another 5000 metres to satisfy his political and sporting directors and understandably took things easy - for him - with a time of 14:18.8.

For the 10,000 metres at the European Championships in Brussels on 23 August there were only 14 entries. The Finns and Swedes, who might well have been excused for being resigned to defeat, sent only one athlete each. They were Koskela and Albertsson respectively, who had lost to Zátopek before and had no hope of matching his times. Heino was still competing but had not been selected. Only Belgium, France and Yugoslavia sent two representatives. They could all have had a dozen each, if the rules had allowed. It would have made no difference to the result.

The weather was awful. There had been a heavy thunderstorm before the start. The track was in poor condition, soft and covered with puddles. Zátopek appeared not to notice such trifling inconveniences. He tolerated the slow pace for a lap then went away on his own. He ran successive laps of the oddly-built 449.29-metre track in 74, 76, 77, 77, 77, 77, 77, 78, 78, 78, 79, 77, 78, 78, 77, 77, 79, 78, 77, 78, 69. He passed 5000m in 14:37.0, exactly as he had done in his World record at Turku, and then seemed content to concentrate on the absorbing task of lapping everyone else. Alain Mimoun, of France, was 2nd, as he had been at Wembley. Koskela was 3rd. The AAA six miles champion, Frank Aaron, beat the British record in 4th place. Albertsson retired at halfway.

The 5000 metres heats took place the following evening, and Zátopek, Mimoun and Albertsson were the only contestants from the 10,000 to start again. Among the 16 competitors were Reiff, running in front of his home crowd, and the Finns, Mäkelä and Posti, who had achieved times of 14:20.2 and 14:20.4 in a race a fortnight previously. These two would actually remain the 2nd and 3rd fastest performers in the World at the distance for the year, but Zátopek had already run better than that in four races since June. With only four men to be eliminated the heats were of no great consequence to anyone other than a Greek named Vasilios Havrapostoulos who set a national record of 15:08.4 behind Zátopek's winning 14:56.0.

The final was two days later, on 26 August. It was naturally viewed by the Belgian press and by the 60,000 people in the stadium as a Reiff-v-Zátopek contest, as had been the case at Wembley, and just as at Wembley Zátopek had already won the 10,000 and Mimoun had been 2nd. Reiff had won the Wembley 5000 in the most enthralling circumstances, and Koskela, Mäkelä and Albertsson had also run in that race. History was being primed to repeat itself, and it was said that Reiff believed he was ready to run 14:03 and write out the same result as before.

He certainly set out as if he intended to do just that. He ran the first kilometre in 2:48.0, which was 14min pace, and continued at much the same rate. Reiff always led, sometimes gaining as much as 10 metres. Zátopek, having moved up in the third lap as was his custom, always followed and retrieved every brief advantage that Reiff had forced. Successive kilometres were run in 2:49.6, 2:49.8 and 2:50.4, and though it was fast it was simply not fast enough. Zátopek led with 1500 metres to go, and when Reiff took over again Zátopek was still on his heels at the bell, and it was Zátopek and not Reiff who found that the 14:03 was there in his legs on the day. The Czech thundered away to a crushing victory. Reiff cracked completely and was passed for the silver medal by the patient Mimoun.

Zátopek had not been well before the Championships and had been in hospital for treatment of a stomach disorder. Maybe the rest did him good! As Peter Lovesey wrote in his book, "Zátopek's running in Brussels was sublime. I doubt whether he ever displayed more withering superiority over all opposition."

The facts were now plain for everyone to see. In the course of these European Championships Zátopek had demonstrated beyond any remaining shadow of doubt his consummate skills as a distance runner. At 10,000 metres he had outclassed the rest from the earliest stages of the race, and even with the prospect of two more hard races to come he had galloped on alone to a time which would have been a World record a month before. At 5000 metres he had followed the relentless pace set by one of the World's best runners of his generation against the clock, and he had destroyed him at the climax, finishing in the second fastest time in history.

10,000 metres: 1 Zátopek (Czechoslovakia) 29:12.0, 2 Mimoun (France) 30:21.0, 3 Koskela (Finland) 30:30.8, 4 Aaron (GB) 30:31.6, 5 Popov (USSR) 30:34.4, 6 Stokken (Norway) 30:44.8, 7 van de Wattyne (Belgium) 30:48.6, 8 Cosgül (Turkey) 30:50.0, 9 Doms (Belgium) 31:04.2, 10 Stefanovic (Yugoslavia) 31:20.0, 11 Mihalic (Yugoslavia) 31:29.2, 12 Petitjean (France) 32:04.4. Did not finish: Albertsson (Sweden), Coll (Spain).

5000 metres: 1 Zátopek (Czechoslovakia) 14:03.0, 2 Mimoun (France) 14:26.0, 3 Reiff (Belgium) 14:26.2, 4 Koskela (Finland) 14:30.8, 5 Posti (Finland) 14:40.8, 6 Theys (Belgium) 14:42.4, 7 Pavlovic (Yugoslavia) 14:50.2, 8 Olney (GB) 14:51.8, 9 Djuraskovic (Yugoslavia) 14:52.4, 10 Albertsson (Sweden) 15:02.2, 11 B. Karlsson (Sweden) 15:09.4. Did not finish: Jacques Vernier (France).

His gold medal double was not the only cause for satisfaction for Zátopek. Though Dana had been beaten into 5th place in the javelin, a long-time clubmate, Jindrich Roudný, won the steeplechase. Roudný had lost on numerous occasions to Zátopek at various distances over the years but had clearly benefited from the painful lessons. In Prague on 30-31 August Zátopek scored a double in the match against Finland to remind the Finns - if they needed reminding - that their time was past. He won the 10,000 metres by almost one and a half minutes in 29:54.6 and the next day ran another brilliant 5000 metres in 14:05.2, despite suffering a muscle injury, with the Finns coming in over three-quarters of a minute down. He still managed to get in two more races at 10,000 metres in the next couple of weeks and finished off the year with three races at 5000 metres and another at 10,000, all in modest times by his standards, during October.

Writing in "The Kings of Distance", Peter Lovesey had these keenly chosen words to say about the position that Zátopek now found himself in: "The long distance runner's loneliness has become proverbial. He is not a melancholy ascetic, though. The hours of his training, the years of persistence, are directed towards the achievement of solitude, in a rare and exquisite form. He craves the ecstasy of outstripping all runners, darting clear of the group into his own dimension of speed and stamina, to set standards unapproached by other men. If he ever achieves such blissful isolation, a runner will do well to savour it, for the experience is transient. Anyone who ventures to surpass a previous limit of human achievement must expect to be followed by others who respond to the revelation of new possibilities.

"In 1950 Emil Zátopek so manifestly set himself apart from other distance runners that reporters described events in which he participated as separate races: one for Zátopek, the other for those who struggled far behind for 2nd place. The search for a metaphor to convey his surplus of energy produced 'The Human Locomotive'; but Zátopek and his aspiring rivals knew that it would be truer to describe him as a hare, agile and elusive, but certain in time to be caught."

As yet, there was still a lot of catching up for the others to do. In 1950 Zátopek had been invincible. He had won two major Championships in a manner which had only been matched by Paavo Nurmi and his Olympic double at 1500 and 5000 metres on the same afternoon in 1924. He had run the seven fastest times of the year at 5000 metres, including the second, third and fourth fastest ever. He had run the seven fastest times of the year at 10,000 metres, including a World record and the second fastest ever. Had the timekeepers in Turku been alert to their task, he would have had another World record at six miles.

At 5000 metres Zátopek had broken 14:20 on seven occasions. Nobody else had at all. There were two promising Finns, Posti at 14:20.4 and Taipale at 14:29.4, though they had a great deal to live up to. There was a German, Schade, who had run 14:22.8 but had not appeared in Brussels, and was in any case already 28 years of age. Much further down the lists a number of Soviet runners were beginning to achieve reasonable times, and one of them - Kazantsev, Pozhidayev, Semyonov, Yevseyev, Alekseyev, Anufriyev - might in the fullness of time make the half-minute improvement needed to begin to match the elusive Czech hare. Reiff, 8th fastest in the World, and Heino, 13th fastest, seemed to have shot their bolt. Great Britain still had nobody within a quarter-of-a-minute of Wooderson's three-mile record.

ZÁ-TO-PEK! ZÁ-TO-PEK! ZÁ-TO-PEK!

At 10,000 metres, there were two World Lists, just as there were so often two 10,000 metres races within one. Zátopek led his own private list of sub-30min clockings. Semyonov, of the USSR, led the rest at 30:07.0. His compatriot, Vanin, had run 30:09.6 but was now 36 years of age and maybe had a future in the marathon. Schade had run 30:10.6 late in the year. There were no Finns in the top 10. Frank Aaron was the only Briton in the top 50.

7.

NEW CHALLENGES IN 1951

A man of flying feet one moment and dragging limbs the next

FROM 1951 ONWARDS "Athletics Weekly" began to carry regular reports from Prague by the British-born journalist, J. Armour Milne, who was the correspondent there for the "Daily Worker" newspaper. Milne had led an interesting life as an athlete, a coach and a journalist, and had become a Communist by conviction. In the "cold war" atmosphere of that Stalinist era of the early 1950s this inevitably meant that his articles were treated with some suspicion in the West, even when they were concerned with purely sporting matter. This was undeserved because Milne was an imaginative and skilled writer who spoke both Czech and Russian and found himself in the enviable position of being on hand for all of Emil Zátopek's record-breaking achievements.

Milne had been a fine sprinter in the 1920s and 1930s and had competed regularly as a professional at Highland Games meetings and in the annual Powderhall Handicaps in Edinburgh. He was already then a journalist by profession, working for the "Sporting Life", and in 1938, at the age of 35 and presumed to be past his best as an athlete, he had scored a controversial win off 15 yards in the 130 yards Powderhall race. He ran under the name of "E.J. Saxon" and his unexpected success caused a great deal of disgruntlement among those who lost bets on the outcome.

One of his first reports in "Athletics Weekly" was based on an enterprising interview with Dr Zdenek Hornof, who had closely followed Zátopek's career for the previous seven years and had carried out regular tests and medical checks to guarantee the great runner's fitness. It could have been no glad tidings for "AW" readers, who were perhaps hoping that Zátopek's phenomenal successes would be explained by the fact that he was some sort of physical freak, that Dr Hornof assured Milne that Zátopek's heart and lungs were no bigger than those of any other outstanding athletes and that his pulse rate was an unexceptional 68. Zátopek's common human frailties were made further evident when it was revealed that he had collided with a tree while out ski-ing, had torn a ligament, and now had his leg in plaster and would not be able to resume training until April.

Because of his late start Zátopek was restricted in his efforts during the track season. He began well enough with an 8:17.6 for 3000 metres on 2 June, which was not far off the best he had achieved for that event the previous year, but in Prague on 11 July he was beaten in a slow race at the same distance by Václav Cevona. It was hardly an unlikely result because Cevona ranked in the top dozen 1500 metres runners in the World, but it was the first time that Zátopek had lost to a fellow Czech since 1944! According to Kozík, it came as no surprise to the vanquished champion who knew that he was in indifferent form, but others in Czechoslovakia got excited enough about it that the Army even reorganised his duties so that he could train during the daytime.

Without being pressed, he ran a series of commendable 5000-metre times, with a best of 14:11.6 in Berlin on 18 August, and even there he won by 40 seconds. At 10,000 metres he waited until the match against Hungary in Budapest on 25 August to make his season's debut and won that (by well over two minutes) in 30:01.4. He knocked off three more races at the distance in the next four weeks, including a splendid 29:29.8 at Trebíc on 1 September, which was actually his fifth best ever for the event. It was only then, by Kozík's reckoning, that Zátopek decided he would venture into new territory and challenge the World records at 20,000 metres and one hour held by Viljo Heino. In 1945 Heino had completed 19,339 metres in the hour to beat Nurmi's previous record from 1928. In 1949 Heino had run 1hr 2min 40.0sec for 20,000 metres.

The record attempt was set up for the Strahov Stadium in Prague on 15 September, and it would be different to anything Zátopek had tried before. The distance, of course, was a new one for him, but the race was going to be incorporated into the 5000 metres event at the Army championships and Zátopek would thus have company, and maybe even some pacemaking assistance, for a small part of the way. Zátopek set himself a target of 1:02:30 which entailed 75sec per lap for 50 laps.

J. Armour Milne only got to hear of the record attempt three days beforehand, and it was fortunate he was able to be there because he provided a wonderfully vivid description of the event for "AW" readers. By the time the 5000 metres - and the World record attempt - started there had been a succession of races at 200, 400 and 800 metres and the track was not in the best of condition. Milne wrote the following:

"He ran as only Zátopek could run such a distance. One moment he was looking like a super-tuned machine, the next like a fugitive from justice: grimacing painfully in one lap, smiling contentedly in the next, and finally winding up with a last lap that would have done credit to a first-class miler. This was the Zátopek the World knows, biting at the distance in snatches, a man of flying feet one moment, dragging limbs the next. There were times when he really looked as if he would provide a real sensation by retiring. Then a deep breath that seemed to lift him six inches taller sent him on his way again, refreshed and bubbling over with pace.

"At 16 kilometres one began to sympathise with him. He gave every appearance of being distressingly uncomfortable. With another kilometre behind him he looked as if he would welcome a lift. Yet only a lap later something appeared to have cheered him immensely for he turned on a full-power grin that brought an appreciative yell from a packed grandstand."

What powerful imagery those words conjur up! For those who were ever privileged, if only once in their lives, to have seen Zátopek in action the description would be immediately familiar and bring a nostalgic smile to the lips.

As might have been expected the 5000 metres runners were not of great help to Zátopek. He was already 100 metres further round the track when the winner finished! Even so, the great man was in the process of exercising remarkable restraint in adhering as doggedly as he could to his schedule. He had aimed for 31:45 at 10,000 metres and he went through in 31:05. Having assured himself of how easy that was, he then sped off over the second half in 30:10.8. He passed Heino's hour mark with still more than half-a-minute or so to spare and got to 19,558 metres before the clock struck. He went on to 20,000 metres in 1:01:15.8, to beat Heino's record by almost a minute-and-a-half. It would suffice for the time being - well, to be precise, for a fortnight, no more.

Zátopek had immediately decided he could do much better, and another attack was arranged for 29 September at the Houštka Spa track at Stará Boleslav which Milne evocatively described as "a sort of transposed Motspur Park"- the leafy suburban Surrey setting for Sydney Wooderson's pre-war World records at the half-mile and mile. Quite what Zátopek's targets were on this occasion is not apparent, but he had put himself in the unusual position of attacking his own record for once, instead of somebody else's. Milne, having dealt with the previous race at such lyrical length, wisely elected to confine himself to the facts on this occasion, and the facts were bold enough to speak for themselves. Running with marvellous judgment on the unconventional 363.78-metre circuit, Zátopek produced successive 5000-metre "splits" of 14:57.4, 14:56.0, 15:01.2 and 14:57.1 (two halves of 29:53.4 and 29:58.4) for a 20,000 metres time of 59:51.8. He broke Heino's 10 miles record by 70 seconds en route with 48:12.0 and he completed an historic 20,052 metres in the hour.

J. Armour Milne, again watching intently and excitedly from the stands, worked out that Zátopek had run successive six-mile stretches in 28:51.8 and 29:04.4. "In cold figures," reported Milne, "this means that if Zátopek had run against the two best six-milers Britain has ever had he would have been 130 yards ahead of Hesketh and 230 yards ahead of Pirie at six miles. And with these two retiring, he would have gone on to reel off another six miles at almost the same pace".

Zátopek was swamped by congratulatory athletes and officials as he finished, and in the words of Milne, "came out of the scrum shoulder-high. He was carried across the field to the front of the grandstand, as the race had started and finished on the back straight, and there he gave a racy speech on radio and through the loudspeakers. And not once by even the smallest hesitation did he betray the fact that he had belted the living daylight out of two tremendous World records". Dr Hornof was on hand to force his way through the crowd and record that Zátopek's pulse rate, which had been 58 per minute before the race, was 168 immediately after. It reduced to 108 after four minutes, 98 after 10 minutes, and 52 after three hours.

Dr Hornof, quizzed again about his protégé's physical attributes, enthused about the "astonishing capacity of Zátopek's blood circulation to make great efforts and bring on very little fatigue". Apparently, Zátopek could perform 30 knee-bends in 30 seconds or three minutes' running at 180 strides per minute and his pulse rate would still be back to 60 within a minute. Without even knowing what that meant precisely in terms of running World-record times on a track, it sounded dauntingly impressive.

Zátopek's World records at 10 miles, one hour and 20,000 metres - kilometre by kilometre:

Strahov Stadium, Prague, 15 September

3:04.7 6:13.0 9:21.2 12:37.0 15:35.6 18:43.0 21:48.0 24:52.8 27:59.6 31:05.0
34:07.8 37:08.8 40:09.4 43:12.8 46:14.0 49:17.0 52:18.2 55:20.0 58:23.0 1:01:16

Houstka Spa Stadium, Stará Boleslav, 29 September

2:58.0 5:55.0 8:56.2 11:56.4 14:57.4 17:57.4 20:56.0 23:55.0 26:53.2 29:53.4
32:52.0 35:51.0 38:52.0 41:52.0 44:54.6 47:56.0 50:56.2 53:58.0 57:00.0 59:51.8

Zátopek now held the World records at 10,000 metres, 10 miles, one hour and 20,000 metres. All of these records had previously been set by Nurmi and Heino and their respective performances make interesting reading:

	10,000 m	10 miles	One hour	20,000 m
Nurmi	30:06.2	50:15.0	19,210 metres	1:04:38.4
Heino	29:35.4	49:22.2	19,339 metres	1:02:40.0
Zátopek	29:02.6	48:12.0	20,052 metres	59:51.8

Jimmy Green gave his considered assessment of the implications of the new World records in a subsequent issue of "Athletics Weekly": "It has been proved beyond question that the fast-slow method of training is vastly superior to any other for getting the best out of the average athlete. Practically all the famous distance-runners, whatever their nationality, use this kind of training to condition themselves nowadays, and the results achieved are reflected in the recent amendments to the record-books. Not, let it be mentioned, by the amazing feats of Zátopek alone, but by the very great improvement in the standards of most countries at the distances".

Considering that Green would not have had access to detailed statistical summaries for the year, this was a bold and brave statement, but an examination of the ranking lists over a four-year period (which were only put together in retrospect as a consequence of diligent research many years afterwards) shows that he was right in his evaluation. This can be seen from the following table:

Comparative World rankings for 10,000 metres 1948 to 1951:

Year	10th ranking	25th ranking	50th ranking
1948	30:29.6	31:10.7	31:44.6
1949	30:38.4	31:11.4	31:39.8
1950	30:28.6	30:58.0	31:29.0
1951	30:21.8	30:44.8	31:16.6

Despite his relatively quiet summer Zátopek had produced three of the five fastest times of the year at 5000 metres. Gaston Reiff, still only 30 after all, had run the year's best of 14:10.8 in Brussels in June. Herbert Schade, of Germany, had made a further advance to 14:15.4. Nikifor Popov, though 40 years of age, had reduced the Soviet record to 14:20.8. Albertsson, Koskela, Posti, Mimoun, Stokken and Kazantsev came next, so there was no obvious new star in the making there. Three Britons - Roy Beckett, Chris Chataway and Gordon Pirie - had got within 10 seconds of Wooderson's three-mile record, which was progress of a sort, and Chataway and Pirie were both only 20 years of age.

At 10,000 metres Zátopek's 29:29.8 was good enough to lead by a wide margin, and there were only two men who had run 10,000 metres faster than the first half of Zátopek's 20,000 metres World record in Stará

Boleslav: Schade, with 29:42.2, and Albertsson, with 29:46.0. The Britons, Walter Hesketh and Gordon Pirie, should not have felt too downcast by J. Armour Milne's invidious comparison of their best six-mile performances with Zátopek's intermediate times. Hesketh had run the equivalent of a top 10 time at 10,000 metres and Pirie the equivalent of a top 15.

8.

OLYMPIC YEAR OF 1952

The "infernal test" is reduced, it seems, to a stroll down the street

IT SEEMS DIFFICULT to believe now, but by the time the Olympic Games were imminent in the summer of 1952 Emil Zátopek was by no means the clear favourite for any of the gold medals in the distance events, let alone all three. He had not had the best of preparations during the preceding months, and it seemed as if others - having learned of his training methods a couple of years before and decided to copy them - were now beginning to feel the long-term benefit.

Zátopek went down with influenza early in the year, tried to get back into training too soon, and struggled to find form when he did start running properly again. His first results were not encouraging: 8:32.4 for 3000 metres in April, 14:46.4 for 5000 metres in Prague on 21 May, 30:08.8 for 10,000 metres in Leipzig on 30 May. By June he had improved, as he had to, but his first major test of the season showed him how much work there was still to catch up on.

He went to Kiev, presumably by command, to take on the Soviet's leading runners in the USSR-Czechoslovakia match and on the first day, 11 June, was soundly beaten at 5000 metres by Vladimir Kazantsev and Nikifor Popov. Kazantsev ran a national record 14:13.2, Popov 14:16.0, and Zátopek only 14:22.0. It was the first time he had lost in 50 races at 5000 metres since being beaten by Gaston Reiff in 1948. The next day he ran the 10,000 against Aleksandr Anufriyev, who attacked him from the start and led by 120 metres after only two kilometres. Zátopek eventually got back to him and valiantly won in 29:26.0, but Anufriyev hung on to finish in 29:31.4. This was a massive improvement on his 1951 best of

30:53.0 and only Zátopek and Heino had ever run faster. Three days later in France Alain Mimoun was to set a national record of 29:38.2.

Zátopek went a bit faster at 5000 metres in the Czech championships on 27 June, winning in 14:17.6, but in the meantime the German, Herbert Schade, had come right into the main reckoning for the Helsinki Olympics with a 14:06.6 - third best all-time to Hägg and Zátopek - and in the USSR Kazantsev had improved to 14:08.8 and Anufriyev to 14:12.2. At the Whitsun holiday Inter-Counties' Championships at the White City, Gordon Pirie had at last beaten Wooderson's British record for three miles with 13:44.8, and Frank Sando (like Pirie only 21 years old) had not been far behind in 13:48.0. Those most astute of observers, the McWhirter twins, in their "Athletics World" account, calculated that Pirie was still seven yards a lap slower than Zátopek at his best for 5000 metres. However, it would seem that Zátopek, with less than a month to go to the Olympics, was not at his best.

J. Armour Milne, reporting on the Czech championships, wrote: "So far as the Olympic Games are concerned I fancy that Emil Zátopek will not be as good as he was in London four years ago. It is always difficult to judge any performance by the amazing Zátopek, but I must say that I didn't like the way he ran in Prague, even if he did all that one could normally ask of him, winning the 5000 metres by 150 yards and the 10,000 metres by half a lap. In both races he looked even more uncomfortable than is his wont, and in the longer race he seemed even to be shocked by the fact that he was not drawing away from the second man as quickly as he seemed to expect to or want to."

The expert forecasts of Olympic winners published in the July 1952 issue of "Athletics World" reflected the general lack of belief in Zátopek's readiness, at least at 5000 metres, among the World's leading statisticians: Dr Roberto Quercetani (Italy) - Schade. Dr Donald Potts (USA) - Reiff. Ekkehard zur Megede (Germany) - Schade. Fulvio Regli (Switzerland) - Schade. Norris & Ross McWhirter (GB) - Zátopek..

At 10,000 metres there was greater confidence in the World record-holder and only zur Megede, choosing Schade again, did not back Zátopek to win. Roberto Quercetani and the McWhirter twins must have known something the others didn't, because they also had Zátopek down to win the marathon if he decided to run it.

ZÁ-TO-PEK! ZÁ-TO-PEK! ZÁ-TO-PEK!

František Kozík remained ideologically cheerful about Zátopek's disposition: "If one just looked at the results, then one had to admit that his prospects were less good than they had been before the Games held in London, but if we made allowance for our great hopes in him and his well-proven human qualities and sportsmanship, then we could look forward to the hard struggles to be encountered in Helsinki with more confidence than ever before. Zátopek had never let us down yet!"

Jimmy Green, in "Athletics Weekly", pronounced of the 5000 metres that "Chataway has a great chance and Reiff, Zátopek, Pirie, Schade and Mimoun should all be there." Joe Binks, the veteran ex-miler now writing for the "News of the World", loftily informed Roberto Quercetani, when the maestro of athletics journalists inquired of him what he thought of Zátopek's chances, that Chataway would win and Pirie was the only one who could challenge him - though that might have been ironic English humour!

Zátopek arrived at the Olympic village at Otaniemi on 11 July, nine days before the 10,000 metres was due to take place, and promptly went out to the track and ran 30 x 400 metres. The next day he ran 40 x 400 metres. Then he gradually reduced his daily mileage. Zátopek must have been well aware that he was not in the form he would have liked to have been in, but he was back in a city which had happy memories for him, and he was to race in front of a knowledgable Finnish crowd which had the highest regard for him. He had run inside 29:30 for 10,000 metres in June, and no one else among his competitors ever had. The 10,000 metres came first. Only after that would it be time to turn attention to the 5000 metres.

On the evening of 20 July there were 70,000 spectators in Helsinki's Olympic Stadium, including the legendary old runners, Hannes Kolehmainen and Paavo Nurmi. There were 33 starters for the 10,000 metres. The vast majority came from Europe, but there were two from the USA and one each from Australia, Chile, Guatemala, Pakistan, South Africa and Vietnam. The fastest among them were the following:

Zátopek (Czechoslovakia) 29:02.6, Anufriyev (USSR) 29:31.4, Mimoun (France) 29:38.2, Albertsson (Sweden) 29:46.0, Stokken (Norway) 29:55.0, Posti (Finland) 30:05.2, Koskela (Finland) 30:10.0, Mihalic

(Yugoslavia) 30:10.0, Nyström (Sweden) 30:11.0, Popov (USSR) 30:23.8, Karlsson (Sweden) 30:25.2, Stone (USA) 30:33.4. At six miles (equivalent to about 1min slower for 10,000 metres) - Pirie (GB) 28:55.6, F. Norris (GB) 29:00.6, Sando (GB) 29:05.2, Perry (Australia) 29:18.4. A notable non-starter was Schade, presumably saving himself for the 5000 metres.

The early pace was set by Anufriyev, just as he had done against Zátopek in June in Kiev, and at 2000 metres the time was 5:51.0. Zátopek went ahead after that and led at halfway in 14:43.4 (29:28 pace), with Mimoun, Pirie, Perry, Anufriyev, Sando and Posti following. Zátopek increased the tempo, running the next kilometre stretches in 2:56 and 2:55 and only Mimoun was able to follow him. Three laps from the finish the French-Algerian finally had to let Zátopek go, and a last 400 metres in 64sec brought Zátopek home in an Olympic record 29:17.0. Only he had ever run faster, and it was a stunning demonstration of yet another facet of the Czech's seemingly unlimited capabilities.

Peter Lovesey, intrigued by what he wittily described as the "Sancho Panza" role played by Zátopek's shadow, wrote of the middle stages of the race: "Mimoun had developed his innate facility for running by training to Zátopek's formula, and his untroubled stride suggested that he was the likeliest adversary to survive the murderous bursts of speed which the Czech could now be expected to introduce. But, perversely, Zátaopek ran with the evenness of a metronome, just fractionally faster than the earlier laps. His challengers successively slipped away, until only the Frenchman had not conceded defeat".

It had been what the eminent French journalist, Gaston Meyer, called "the pitiless race of elimination", and even in the process of being thoroughly beaten the other runners had contributed to the greatest 10,000 metres contest in history. Before the start only eight men had ever run faster than 30 minutes, and only the pioneers, Máki and Heino, and the German, Schade, were absent on the day. In the race six men finished inside 30 minutes. Mimoun set a national record in 2nd place. Posti became the second fastest Finn ever (to Heino) in 4th place, even though for the first time in Olympic history no Scandinavian won a medal. Sando beat the British record in 5th place. Nyström improved over a quarter-of-a-minute in 6th place. The McWhirters also pointed out that Pirie, in 7th place, would have joined the select sub-30 company "had he not played with fire in trying to tease the mighty Zátopek in the middle stages".

For the 5000 metres heats held two days later on 22 July there were 45 entries from 24 countries. Again, as one would expect, they were mostly from Europe, but Australia, Canada, Iran, Japan, New Zealand and the USA were also represented, and two of the three Frenchmen had been born in North Africa. The fastest in the field were the following:

Zátopek (Czechoslovakia) 14:03.0, Schade (Germany) 14:06.6, Reiff (Belgium) 14:10.8, Anufriyev (USSR) 14:12.2, Koskela (Finland) 14:13.2, Popov (USSR) 14:16.0, Semyonov (USSR) 14:18.2, Albertsson (Sweden) 14:20.8, Mimoun (France) 14:21.8, Kovács (Hungary) 14:23.6, Stokken (Norway) 14:23.8, Ceraj (Yugoslavia) 14:26.2, Pavlovic (Yugoslavia) 14:26.6, Stone (USA) 14:27.0. At three miles (equivalent to about 30sec slower at 5000 metres) - Pirie (GB) 13:44.8, Chataway (GB) 13:59.6, Parker (GB) 14:00.8, Perry (Australia) 14:02.0

Popov, Kovács, Semyonov, Ceraj, Stokken, Stone and Koskela were all eliminated in succession in the three heats, as were an Australian, John Landy, and an American, Wes Santee, whose best was yet to come in pursuit of the first sub-four-minute mile. Zátopek was in fine humour, remonstrating with Anufriyev for setting off too fast, chatting away to Chataway, and then slowing down to encourage the American, Curt Stone. In the last lap Zátopek cheerfully urged Anufriyev on to victory and was content to amble in at his leisure with Albertsson, Perry and Chataway in the other qualifying places, well ahead of the sixth man, Ib Planck, of Denmark, who was no doubt happy enough with a national record to his name. Such nonchalance from Zátopek spelled out a stark message for his rivals. He was back to form, happy and confident.

The finalists were Zátopek, Perry (Australia), Reiff, Theys (both Belgium), Taipala, Tuomaala (both Finland), Mimoun (France), Schade (Germany), Pirie, Chataway, Parker (all Great Britain), Béres (Hungary), Albertsson, Andersson (both Sweden) and Anufriyev (USSR). Personal bests had been set in the heats by all of them except Zátopek, Reiff,

Schade, Albertsson and Anufriyev. Most notably, Parker had run 14:18.2, Mimoun 14:19.0 and Béres 14:19.6.

The final took place at 4.40 on the afternoon of 24 July. Schade, perhaps unwisely, is supposed to have asked Zátopek just before the start who he thought was his most dangerous opponent and Zátopek, with great presence of mind, replied, "Reiff", which presumably left the German perplexed as to whether that meant that Zátopek simply didn't think much of him or was merely under-rating him.

Whatever frame of mind he was in, the German set off at a very brisk pace. He led at 1000 metres from Mimoun, Reiff, Chataway, Parker and Zátopek (biding his time, as usual) in 2:47.0 - which, if maintained, would produce a World record 13:55. At 2000 metres Schade still led at only a slightly slower speed. Zátopek and Pirie both briefly went ahead, but Schade was in front at 3000 and 4000 metres, having run progressively slower kilometre "splits" of 2:50.4, 2:53.0 and 2:54.4. At the bell Schade led from Chataway, Mimoun and Zátopek. Pirie was a little further back, while the nerves of Reiff, the defending champion, had failed him again and he had dropped out. The McWhirters described the closing stages as follows in "Athletics World":

"With 300 metres to go Chataway forged into the lead, and for several fleeting moments it looked as though he could win. Entering the last turn Zátopek, Mimoun and Schade all rallied for a final assault. Just past the crown of the bend Zátopek made a decisive attack just as Mimoun was passing Schade, who in turn was fighting it out with Chataway. Suddenly the vast crowd, who were already in an uproar, let out a bellow, for the Englishman lay sprawled across the concrete curb. Brushed perhaps, but not barged, he was tired enough to trip over a blade of grass. Zátopek, who by now had really let in the clutch, stormed up the straight to complete his last lap in a prodigious 57.9sec, and so to win by five yards".

This was yet another surprise sleight of hand from a Zátopek repertoire of magical tricks which would have occupied an entire "Sunday Night at the London Palladium". Having won races in the past with relentless pace from the starting gun, or with irresistible surges along the way, or with subtle increases of tempo which were hardly noticed until they bit home, he now had produced, like a rabbit out of a hat, a last lap which was just about as fast as he could expect to run were his schedule that day to require only a single 400 metres flat-out time-trial.

As had happened at 10,000 metres, the 5000 metres in Helsinki was the most competitive race ever run at the distance. Mimoun, dubbed the "Silver Phantom" by the McWhirters, broke another national record in 2nd place. Schade, having made much of the pacemaking, was under 14:09 for the bronze medal. Pirie and Chataway, though 60 metres back, both ran personal bests. Anufriyev, assessed by Gaston Meyer as "a good worker rather than an artist of the track", finished a distant 10th.

Meyer, viewing the race from a French perspective, interestingly described it as "not a conclusion but a point of departure". He pointed out that all three medallists were primarily 10,000 metres runners, and that Mimoun's basic speed was even less than Zátopek's - 3:57.0 for 1500 metres, 8:24.0 for 3000 metres. Reiff, despite his Olympic gold in 1948, had never been a great 5000 metres runner, in Meyer's estimation. The two other candidates for victory in Helsinki, Pirie and Chataway, were still young and lacked maturity. Hägg's World record, "*établi dix ans avant*" (Meyer's italics), was still almost 10 seconds quicker than Zátopek or Mimoun had run to win their medals, and Hägg could have run 13:50, and certainly no worse than 13:55, if pushed.

Meyer's implication is clear. The future at 5000 metres did not lie with the medallists but with the young pretenders. Further, he believed that Mimoun, and not Zátopek, should have won that day. "Mimoun let go a unique opportunity to be Olympic champion," Meyer later wrote. "It is certain by any logic that he could have won if he had taken his chance two laps from the end. Zátopek was in difficulty at that stage and could have been left behind. Chataway, as was shown by his fall, could not hold out for another lap, and Schade lacked the speed for the final sprint. It's easy to reason that way after a race. Who can know? Mimoun's best time on the eve of the final was 14:19. He improved 12 seconds in one race, and who could ask for more? Yet he could have been Olympic champion in 14:05."

Contrary to popular belief, Dana did not quite win her Olympic javelin gold at precisely the same time as husband Emil was earning his in the 5000 metres. Her event started after the 5000 had finished, and

Emil had time for only a brief word of encouragement before leaving the stadium. It is also a fanciful notion that Emil decided to run the marathon simply because he felt the two-to-one margin he now held over his wife in the family contest for Helsinki gold medals was not decisive enough for his liking!

Quite at what juncture Zátopek did make up his mind to definitely take part in the marathon in Helsinki is not clear. There had been suggestions before the Games that because he was unhappy with his form at 5000 metres he might replace that with the marathon. Experts like Quercetani and the McWhirters certainly thought it was possible. Kozík, in his biography, gives no clue. The veteran Slovak journalist, Ladislav Krnác, reckons the idea had been formulated almost a year before and that the two successful 20,000 metres record attempts the previous Autumn had been a sort of dress rehearsal.

In a heartfelt tribute to Zátopek after his death which Krnác wrote for the magazine published by the International Association of Athletics Federations, he said that it was a senior official of the ATK (Army Sports Club), Lieutenant-Colonel Václav Sabl, who had first proposed the idea to Zátopek of attempting the Olympic triple at 5000 metres, 10,000 metres and the marathon. Lt-Col Sabl reasoned that it was perfectly feasible as Zátopek was already covering 30 kilometres a day in training.

Entries were naturally required to be made in advance of the Games, and Zátopek had been nominated for the marathon by the Czech team management along with Jaroslav Šourek, who had won the national title in June in a respectable 2:37:51.6 and knew Zátopek only too well, having been regularly left far behind him on the track ever since 1947. So it is evident that Zátopek was offered - and accepted - the opportunity at least a month beforehand to run the Olympic marathon.

There were 66 runners on the stadium start line on the afternoon of Sunday 27 July, and they included full contingents from all the traditionally dominant marathon-running nations: Cabrera, Fernández and Gorno, of Argentina; Hietanen, Karvonen and Puolakka, of Finland; Cox, Iden and Peters, of Great Britain; Nishida, Uchikawa and Yamada, of Japan; Chong Oh Hong, Choong Sik Choi and Yoon Chil Choi, of Korea; Hayward, Keith and Luyt, of South Africa. There were 32 nations taking part from all five continents.

ZÁ-TO-PEK! ZÁ-TO-PEK! ZÁ-TO-PEK!

Cabrera had won the Olympic gold in 1948. Hietanen had been European champion in 1946, and Karvonen was 2nd in 1950. Peters had run by far the fastest marathon ever of 2:20:42.2 in June, and Cox had been within a minute of him. Flores, of Guatemala, had won the World's oldest annual marathon in Boston in April. There were others from countries such as Belgium, Hungary, Norway, Rumania and Sweden with slower times but plenty of gritty experience. There were those from Egypt, India and Pakistan who had gained their selections with much more modest performances and would settle for the honour of taking part. There were one or two who had never actually run a marathon, and that minority group included the celebrated Czech No.2.

The story of the race has become familiar legend. Zátopek was "making an experiment", as he put it beforehand, but according to the account by one of the most respected of sportswriters, Willy Meisl, in the British Olympic Association's Official Report of the Games, both the Zátopeks were always confident that he would win, and he ran as to the manner born. A photograph of the competitors as they were still circling the track before setting out on the roads shows that Zátopek was already just behind the leaders, and that's where he stayed, apparently running without any great effort, until he decided to strike out on his own.

Jim Peters, the record-holder, had finished 8th when Zátopek won the 1948 Olympic 10,000 metres and seemed to have decided to run the legs off the Czech from the start. Peters went through 5km in 15:43 (Zátopek 16:02) and 10km in 31:44, which was under 2:15 pace. Zátopek came through with the Swede, Jansson, 28 seconds later, and even they were on target for 2:17. At 15km Peters, Jansson and Zátopek were almost together in 47:58. By 20km (1:04:27) Peters was 10sec down, and maybe dispirited by Zátopek's polite inquiry of him a little earlier as to whether they were running fast enough. Immediately after the halfway turn Zátopek went ahead and, according to the account by Meisl, invited Jansson to run alongside him, but by 30km the Czech double gold-medallist was 26sec clear, with Peters over a minute behind. The McWhirters, with their unfailing knack for a puckish description, suggested of Zátopek that at this stage of the proceedings "unless struck more than once by lightning nothing, it seemed, was going to stop him".

72

Peters and Cox both retired, and heedless of any avenging thunderbolts Zátopek strode on alone and unchallenged. There was none of the familiar head rolling, face twisted into a distraught expression, or agonised glances of Zátopek the track runner. Rather, it seemed as if the man who could beat anybody at 5000 and 10,000 metres, and had already started breaking records at longer distances, had found yet another forte. He ran down the sunlit road, casually looking round as if to admire the suburban scenery and to acknowledge the plaudits of the byestanders, and he appeared to be running well within himself, not wanting to be too presumptuous and humiliate the worthy efforts of the seasoned marathoners trudging along behind him.

Peter Lovesey wrote in "The Kings of Distance": "In the strangest way, Zátopek's arrival dignified and gave point to an occasion that threatened to become as theatrical as a cinema epic. The immensity of the reception, the fanfare, the thunderous applause conventionally demanded a smiling, slightly windblown idol, heroic in stature and movement, modestly acknowledging his due tribute. In reality, the runner who trotted from the darkness of the tunnel appeared mentally removed from the avalanche of emotion that swept down on him. It was as though he alone, of the 70,000 present, realised that he was still competing in an athletic event.

"The mighty Zátopek, whose frenzied sprinting figure, storming to victory among the World's greatest runners, had been pictured that week in millions of newspapers, now appeared a diminutive almost frail man. He was frowning, dazzled perhaps by the glinting sunlight of early evening as he emerged from the tunnel. On his chest the number '903' proclaimed that its wearer was simply one of several thousand men and women who had come to compete in the Games. The short, metallic movements of his legs, devoid of elasticity, spoke of the infernal test to which they had been subjected. His sodden vest, which he had earlier rolled up to the armpits for the blessed freedom of the breeze on his body, now hung loose over his white shorts".

Zátopek smiled as he broke the tape, waved away attendants, and strolled on to the infield to take off his shoes. After a while he ran across to where Dana was seated in the athletes' enclosure and embraced her. It was 2 minutes and 31.8 seconds - which was not much quicker than the time it would take Zátopek to run a kilometre flat out - before the second man, Gorno, crossed the line, and Zátopek hurried across to greet him. Gorno's fellow-Argentinian, Cabrera, came in 6th - the best placing that any defending Olympic champion had ever achieved - and was still over eight minutes faster than when he had won at Wembley. Zátopek had run the third fastest marathon ever, and it almost seemed as if he would have run by far the fastest ever, had he been required to do so to win. Zátopek was truly, as František Kozík had entitled his biography, "The Marathon Victor".

The 1952 Olympic Games: 5000 metres, 10,000 metres, Marathon

10,000 metres (20 July): 1 Zátopek (Czechoslovakia) 29:17.0, 2 Mimoun (France) 29:32.8, 3 Anufriyev (USSR) 29:48.2, 4 Posti (Finland) 29:51.4, 5 Sando (GB) 29:51.8, 6 Nyström (Sweden) 29:54.8, 7 Pirie (GB) 30:04.2, 8 F. Norris (GB) 30:09.8, 9 Pozhidayev (USSR) 30:13.4, 10 Stokken (Norway) 30:22.2, 11 Popov (USSR) 30:24.2, 12 Albertsson (Sweden) 30:34.6, 13 Karlsson (Sweden) 30:35.8, 14 Juhász (Hungary) 30:39.6, 15 Cosgül (Turkey) 30:42.4, 16 Koskela (Finland) 30:43.0, 17 Abdallah Ben Said (France) 30:53.0, 18 Mihalic (Yugoslavia) 30:53.2, 19 Niskanen (Finland) 30:59.6, 20 Stone (USA) 31:02.6, 21 Wilt (USA) 31:04.0, 22 van de Wattyne (Belgium) 31:15.8, 23 Inostroza (Chile) 31:28.6, 24 Thögersen (Denmark) 31:47.8, 25 Mohamed Ben Labidi (France) 31:52.2, 26 Johansson (Iceland) 32:00.0, 27 Perz (Austria) 32:13.2, 28 Keith (South Africa) 32:32.4, 29 van den Rydt (Belgium) 33:13.4, 30 Abdul Rashid (Pakistan) 33:50.4, 31 Velasquez (Guatemala) 35:34.0, 32 Ly Van Tran (Vietnam) 37:33.0. Did not finish: Perry (Australia).

5000 metres (24 July) 1 Zátopek (Czechoslovakia) 14:06.6, 2 Mimoun (France) 14:07.4, 3 Schade (Germany) 14:08.6, 4 Pirie (GB) 14:18.0, 5 Chataway (GB) 14:18.0, 6 Perry (Australia) 14:23.6, 7 Béres (Hungary) 14:24.8, 8 Andersson (Sweden) 14:26.0, 9 Albertsson (Sweden) 14:27.8, 10 Anufriyev (USSR) 14:31.4, 11 Parker (GB) 14:37.0, 12 Taipale (Finland) 14:40.0, 13 Tuomaala (Finland) 14:54.2, 14 Theys (Belgium) 14:59.0. Did not finish: Reiff (Belgium).

Marathon (27 July): 1 Zátopek (Czechoslovakia) 2:23:03.2, 2 Gorno (Argentina) 2:25:35.0, 3 Jansson (Sweden) 2:26:07.0, 4 Yoon Chil Choi (Korea) 2:26:36.0, 5 Karvonen (Finland) 2:26:41.8, 6 Cabrera (Argentina) 2:26:42.4, 7 Dobronyi (Hungary) 2:28:04.8, 8 Puolakka (Finland) 2:29:35.0, 9 Iden (GB) 2:30:42.0, 10 Hayward (South Africa) 2:31:50.2, 11 Luyt (South Africa) 2:32:41.0, 12 Östling (Sweden) 2:32:48.4, 13 Dyrgall (USA) 2:32:52.4, 14 Celedón (Chile) 2:33:45.8, 15 van de Zande (Holland) 2:33:50.0. 16 Olsen (Norway) 2:33:58.4, 17 Hietanen (Finland) 2:34:01.0, 18 de Wachtere (Belgium) 2:34:02.0, 19 Keith (South Africa) 2:34:38.0, 20 Moskachenkov (USSR) 2:34:43.8, 21 Esztergomi (Hungary) 2:35:10.0, 22 Flores (Guatemala) 2:35:40.0, 23 Simonet (Belgium) 2:35:43.0, 24 Kjersem (Norway) 2:36:14.0, 25 Nishida (Japan) 2:36:19.0, 26 Yamada (Japan) 2:38:11.2, 27 Vanin (USSR) 2:38:22.0, 28 Suchkov (USSR) 2:38:28.8, 29 Norrström (Sweden) 2:38:57.4, 30 Engelhardt (Germany) 2:39:37.2. 31 Cristea (Rumania) 2:39:42.2, 32 Leblond (Belgium) 2:40:37.0, 33 Choong Sik Choi (Korea) 2:41:23.0, 34 Systad (Norway) 2:41:29.8, 35 Šourek (Czechoslovakia) 2:41:40.4, 36 Jones (USA) 2:42:50.0, 37 Prentice (Australia) 2:43:13.4, 38 Muhammad Aslam (Pakistan) 2:43:38.2, 39 Gruber (Austria) 2:45.02.0, 40 Collins (Canada) 2:45:58.0, 41 Teodosiu (Rumania) 2:46:00.8, 42 Simonsen (Denmark) 2:46:41.4, 43 Warnemünde (Germany) 2:50:00.0, 44 Corbitt (USA) 2:51:09.0, 45 Smeal (Australia) 2:52:23.0. 46 Bussotti (Italy) 2:52:55.0, 47 Osinski (Poland) 2:54:38.2, 48 Sörensen (Denmark) 2:55:21.0, 49 West (Ireland) 2:56:22.8, 50 Morgenthaler (Switzerland) 2:56:33.0, 51 Hassan Abdel Fattah (Egypt) 2:56:56.0, 52 Surat Singh (India) 2:58:09.2, 53 Berti (Italy) 2:58:36.2.

Did not finish: Aytar (Turkey), Billas (France), Chong Oh Hong (Korea), Cox (GB), Fernández (Argentina), Inostroza (Chile), Krajcar (Yugoslavia), Martufi (Italy), Muhammad Benaras (Pakistan), Peters (GB), Radu (Rumania), Uchikawa (Japan), Velasquez (Guatemala).

9.

MORE WORLD RECORDS IN 1952 AND 1953

"Passing on the great spirit of a champion to the next generation"

HAD EMIL ZÁTOPEK been born 30 years later he could have settled for a lucrative living from big city marathons for the rest of his running life after his Olympic triumphs.

Promoters in Boston, Chicago, New York, London and of the Asahi and Fukuoka events in Japan would have been clamouring for his presence. He would have been pestered with invitations, bombarded with promises of lavish appearance fees, seduced by visions of five-star accommodation, relentlessly pursued by shoe-manufacturers and agents. There would be cosy chats with Presidents and Prime Ministers. He would have become a roving ambassador, feted wherever he went, and Dana would have been always at his side: the pair of them living proof that supreme sporting endeavour could break down political barriers. What Gagarin would achieve for space travel, Zátopek would have done for athletics.

Instead, ever loyal to his supporters and his country, he returned home to a hero's welcome and the next three weeks were taken up with an endless round of receptions and speeches (and training fitted in wherever he could). Eventually, he started a racing tour of the country, winning at 5000 and 10,000 metres in Prague on 14-15 August and then moving on to Gottwaldov (formerly Zlín), Brno, Znojmo, Stará Boleslav and Olomouc, finishing up with another 5000/10,000 double in Warsaw on 27-28 September. None of the 5000s were particularly quick - the best of them was 14:17.8 - but the 10,000 in Warsaw was run in 29:34.0, and the six-week schedule of what were, in effect, exhibition appearances had suited Zátopek's purpose very well as a conditioning programme. He had celebrated his 30th birthday on 19 September and he had in mind further exploits to mark the occasion, as if winning three Olympic gold medals was not enough.

In Opava for the national inter-club championships on 4 October he gave it everything he could in an attempt to beat at long last Hägg's 5000 metres World record of 13:58.2 from 1942. He went through the first kilometre in 2:47.0 and 2000 metres in 5:35.0. This was still eight seconds down on Hägg's schedule, but the Swede had set off at a tremendous pace, and Zátopek remained on course for well inside 14 minutes. At 3000 metres in 8:23.2 the record was under serious threat, but at 4000 metres in 11:17.2 Zátopek was still eight seconds down on Hägg and would need a last kilometre in under 2:41, which was not much slower than he could expect to run in a kilometre race. The final time in the cool of the evening was 14:06.4, and even though the record had survived once more no doubt Schade and Mimoun would have yet again wondered at the resilience of the man, still running in October on his own as fast as he had done for the gold medal in July with them at his heels.

Even so, Zátopek was by no means finished yet for the year. His objective now was another World-record coup: at 15 miles, 25,000 metres and 30,000 metres. The records had been set at the first two distances in the same race in 1948 by Mikko Hietanen, of Finland, at 1:17:28.6 and 1:20:14.0. At 30,000 metres the Soviet runner, Yakov Moskachenkov, had achieved 1:38:54.0 in 1951. In truth, they were not exceptional records. Neither Nurmi nor Heino had ever attempted to set them, and Zátopek only needed to remind himself of the Helsinki marathon to appreciate that these times were at his mercy. He had passed 30 kilometres on that occasion in 1:38:42 and kept going for another 12km-plus. Furthermore, Hietanen had finished 17th in that race and Moskachenkov 20th, both very far behind him.

It would not have been in Zátopek's nature, though, to treat the records with disdain, and in any case he had another opponent to deal with - the early-winter weather. The race was originally arranged for Saturday 25

ZÁ-TO-PEK! ZÁ-TO-PEK! ZÁ-TO-PEK!

October at the forest stadium at Houštka Spa, Stará Boleslav, owned by the Škoda car-manufacturing company, and when Zátopek woke early that morning it was pouring with rain, and it continued to do so for most of the day. It was only because of frantic efforts through the night by the groundsman and his volunteer staff that the track was cleared of water in time for an 11 o'clock start on Sunday morning.

Zátopek had set himself a schedule of 10km splits in 32min, to give him a final time of 1:36 for 30,000 metres. He went through 10km in 31:43, 10 miles in 50:59.8, and the hour mark at 18,970.80 metres. At 20km in 1:03:15.2, he was 45sec inside his schedule, and he went on at what was really a very easy pace for him to set new records of 1:16:26.4 (15 miles), 1:19:11.8 (25,000 metres) and 1:35:23.8 (30,000 metres). There were six other starters, of which the nearest of them finished a quarter-of-an-hour or so later, and all credit to whoever he was (maybe even the faithful Šourek again, who had come in 35th in the Olympic marathon) for accepting the dubious privilege of being lapped 10 times or more!

Zátopek's 5000 metres "splits" were 15:48.0, 15:55.6, 15:51.4, 15:40.2, 16:06.6 and 16:02.0, and it was Šourek who actually led at 10km in 31:24.6. According to J. Armour Milne, it was by no means an uneventful procession. Milne said of Zátopek's aides that they were "trying to get him to keep to some semblance of a schedule, but it just wasn't any good". Maybe Zátopek deliberately varied the tempo to relieve the boredom, because he ran the ninth kilometre, for instance, in 3:17.0 and the 10th in 3:05.6! His 25th kilometre was his slowest at 3:22.6. His 26th was his fastest at 3:01.8! Milne reported that Zátopek was "still full of fire at the finish".

Athletics in Czechoslovakia, inspired by such a fiery example, was buoyant. That same afternoon 21-year-old Stanislav Jungwirth had run 800 metres in 1:48.7, which made him the 7th fastest of all-time. Earlier in the month Jiri Skobla had broken the European record for the shot with 17.12m. In Helsinki Josef Dolezal had won the silver medal in the 50 kilometres walk and in October in Prague he had set new World records for 30 kilometres and two hours.

After the Olympics distance runners in other countries, freed from Zátopek's thrall, had been setting themselves new standards. Gaston Reiff, ever the man for the carefully orchestrated occasion, had broken

MORE WORLD RECORDS IN 1952 AND 1953

Hägg's eight-year-old World record for two miles. The Swede, Nyström, and the German, Schade, had run faster for 10,000 metres than anyone not of Czech nationality. In a year the rankings in this event had been transformed.

WORLD'S BEST OF ALL-TIME AT 10,000 METRES

At the end of 1952:

29:02.6	Emil Zátopek (Czech)	(1)	Turku	04.08.50
29:23.8	Valter Nyström (Sweden)	(1)	Düsseldorf	14.09.52
29:24.8	Herbert Schade (Germany)	(2)	Düsseldorf	14.09.52
29:27.2	Viljo Heino (Finland)	(1)	Kouvola	01.09.49
29:29.4	Alain Mimoun (France)	(1)	Stockholm	04.10.52
29:31.4	Aleksandr Anufriyev (USSR)	(2)	Kiev	12.06.52
29:46.0	Bertil Albertsson (Sweden)	(1)	Uppsala	14.10.51
29:48.4	Öistein Saksvik (Norway)	(1)	Copenhagen	29.08.52
29:48.6	Franjo Mihalic (Yugoslavia)	(1)	Zagreb	04.10.52
29:51.2	Gustaf Jansson (Sweden)	(3)	Düsseldorf	14.09.52

There had been 25 performances at 30min or better during 1952, and both Nyström and Mimoun had been responsible for four of them. Zátopek, for once, was out-numbered with three, but his were the important ones. Altogether there were seven men who had broken 30min for the first time in 1952 - Nyström, Anufriyev, Saksvik, Mihalic, Jansson, Posti and Sando - and Pirie had done the equivalent at six miles. Nyström was already 36, and it might be too late in the day for him to improve yet further. Mihalic was 32, Mimoun 31 and the marathon, runner, Jansson, was 30, but attitudes to age were altering. Saksvik (27), Anufriyev and Posti (both 26) had time on their side. Sando and Pirie, both still 21, might well be maturing into the 1960s.

The euphoria in Czechoslovakia regarding Zátopek's achievements was aptly expressed by one Prague journalist named Mašek who wrote, with Wordsworthian fervour and not the slightest hint of any mundane political message: "The name 'Zátopek' has become synonymous with the idea of speed, endurance, efficiency, reliability, fighting spirit and willpower. It would not surprise me if one day we should find his name in the dictionary as a common expression for all these terms. The delight in work, the conscientiousness, the courage, the feeling of responsibility of a Zátopek should run throughout our whole lives". It was a nice thought - I zatopek, You zatopek, He zatopeks, She zatopeks, We all of us zatopek together!

The late Gordon Pirie, as we know, was one of those young runners of the early 1950s whose whole lives were transformed and uplifted by Zátopek's example. Pirie came from an established running dynasty. His father, Alick, had been a fine athlete who had represented Scotland in the International Cross-Country Championships and had become a stalwart of South London Harriers. Gordon's elder brother, Peter, had been reckoned the more talented one in their youth. Gordon, at the age of 17, had run alongside his father as he helped carry the Olympic torch through the thronged streets towards Wembley Stadium in 1948, and when - after a marvellously tempestuous athletics career - Gordon Pirie came to write his autobiography in 1961, appropriately entitled "Running Wild", he described the occasion with evangelical passion.

"As I waited that sunny morning so long ago I shook with excitement. Then, when my father put the torch in my hand, as if symbolically passing on the great spirit of a champion to the next generation, I was surprised to find it was hot. I ran though the cheering crowds at Reigate, in Surrey, and the flame seemed to draw my very soul on to the start of a great journey down the years. It was the start, too, of a personal crusade to make British athletics match up to the best in the World".

Even so, there was a much more profound experience awaiting the teenage Pirie in the days which immediately followed:

"The event of those Games which really set the seal on my ambitions was the running of Emil Zátopek. I instantly recognised him as the embodiment of an ideal for myself as I saw him scorch through the 10,000 metres field. From that day he has never ceased to be my greatest inspiration and challenge - and my firm friend. My whole life was focussed on the resolve to beat him - and one day I did. Zátopek was a phenomenon and an all-time great.

"That year at Wembley he burst through a mental and physical barrier. He showed runners that what they had been content with up to then was nothing to what could be achieved. They called him 'The

The early days… and already Emil Zátopek is a winner as he brings his technical school road relay team home in 1st place in a race in 1942. He had also taken up track competition, mainly at 1500 metres, and is pictured (below) fifth from the left. He finished 5th in the national championships that year.

Zátopek's first international appearance. At the 1946 European Championships in Oslo, he holds 5th place in the early stages of the 5000 metres behind Raphaël Pujazon (France), Viljo Heino (Finland), Willy Slijkhuis (Holland) and Gaston Reiff (Belgium). The eventual winner, Sydney Wooderson (Great Britain), is in 9th position.

The first gold medal. Zátopek wins the 1948 Wembley Olympic 10,000 metres, and the only other runners in sight are ones he has lapped.

The Wembley Olympic 5000 metres. Zátopek leads in the rain from Gaston Reiff (Belgium) and Erik Ahldén (Sweden). It was Reiff, though, who won in a desperately close finish and Zátopek forever afterwards described his own tactics that day as "very stupid".

The great rivalry. Zátopek beat Alain Mimoun on seven occasions in Championship finals and international matches at 5000 or 10,000 metres until Mimoun won their last encounter in the 1956 Olympic marathon. Here they battle through ankle-deep floods during the 5000 metres at the 1948 France v Czechoslovakia match in Paris. Zátopek, inevitably, was the winner on this occasion, beating his friend and rival by almost a minute.

The Last of the Flying Finns. Zátopek overtakes Viljo Heino to win a pulsating race at 5000 metres in Helsinki in 1947. This was a victory which first endeared Zátopek to the hearts of the knowledgeable Finnish spectators who had seen so many great distance races, and it was to be in Helsinki five years later that he would gain his greatest triumphs.

At the European Championships 5000 metres final in Brussels in 1950
Zátopek overcame another home favourite to win the gold. Gaston
Reiff led the race to the delight of the Belgian crowd, but Zátopek
followed every move and when he attacked in the last lap Reiff
cracked. It was Alain Mimoun, yet again, who came 2nd.

Taking on and beating the
Russians at 5000 metres. Zátopek
leads from Nikifor Popov and
Vladimir Kazantsev in Moscow in
1949. The conditions under which
races were held in that era can
clearly be seen from the ploughed-
up state of the track cinders.

The 1952 Helsinki Olympic 10,000 metres. The early stages pictured from inside and outside the track. Zátopek already leads from Mimoun, Gordon Pirie (GB), Aleksandr Anufriyev (USSR) and Les Perry (Australia). In the photo below the order is Zátopek, Mimoun, Pirie, Perry, Anufriyev, Frank Sando (also GB) and Hannu Posti (Finland). Zátopek and Mimoun were, as always, 1st and 2nd at the finish and Anufriyev took the bronze medal ahead of Posti and Sando.

The dramatic happenings on the last bend of the Helsinki Olympic 5000 metres final. Chris Chataway (GB) falls headlong across the track kerb, while Zátopek speeds away to another gold medal ahead of Alain Mimoun (France) and Herbert Schade (Germany). An hour or so later Dana won the couple's second Olympic title of the day.

Smiling benignly, Zátopek crosses the finishing line in the Helsinki Olympic marathon. It was his debut at the distance and his third gold medal of the Games. Not only that, but he had made it all seem so easy.

Bucharest 1953, and the Eastern Bloc stars gather for the "International World Youth Games". At 5000 metres (above) the Soviet athletes, Vladimir Kuts (leading) and Aleksandr Anufriyev (No. 20), set a tremendous pace from the start, but Zátopek kept them in check, closed the gap, and eventually won the race.
Below: The 10,000 metres was held four days later and Zátopek amiably paced the young Australian, Dave Stephens (No. 255), through the first half of the race before going on to win again. Runner-up in this event was the Hungarian, Jozsef Kovács (No.118).

Many of Zátopek's regular opponents over the years were in the line-up for the 1953 British Games two miles at the White City (above), including Freddie Green (fourth from left), Alain Mimoun (behind No.13), Gaston Reiff (No.12), Chris Chataway (third from right) and Gordon Pirie (far right).

Britain's Gordon Pirie (above) sets the pace in the international two miles race at the 1953 Whitsun British Games from the Belgian, Gaston Reiff, and each had their share of victories and defeats in races against Zátopek. The winner was Chataway (right) in a British record time of 8:49.6. As it happens, this was a distance which Zátopek never had cause to race.

It's still only the first lap of the 1954 European Championships 5000 metres final, but Vladimir Kuts is already flying away from the rest of the field and Emil Zátopek is last but one. Later in the race (below) Zátopek led the pursuing group from Freddie Green (GB), Lucien Hanswijk (Belgium), Herbert Schade (Germany), Jozsef Kovács (Hungary), Chris Chataway (also GB), Frans Herman (also Belgium) and Sándor Garay (Hungary). Kuts was uncatchable and won in a World record time. Chataway was 2nd and Zátopek 3rd.

Gordon Pirie takes a long hard look at Zátopek during the London v Prague 10,000 metres at the White City Stadium, London, in 1955. Pirie, whose athletics career had first been inspired by watching Zátopek at the Wembley Olympics seven years before, won this race, with his team-mate, Ken Norris, 2nd and his idol 3rd.

Zátopek the cross-country runner. Sadly, he never competed in the International Championships, but he often took part in the annual promotion by the newspaper, *L'Humanité*, in Paris. In the 1954 race (pictured here) he runs alongside Vladimir Kuts, and he went on to beat him and other Eastern Bloc stars by a wide margin.

Then, in 1958 at the San Sebastian invitation event, Zátopek followed the North African-born Frenchman, Hamoud Ameur, over the barriers before striding ahead in the later stages to achieve his last major international success.

Coming towards the end of the road. Zátopek takes much-needed refreshment during the 1956 Olympic marathon, but it was his old rival, Alan Mimoun, who was so far ahead that there was even time to allow traffic across the route behind him. At the finish attentive officials, and then Mimoun himself, were there to greet the old champion when he came in 6th.

Even when Zátopek was past his best the competitive flame still burned bright. Here he leads a 5000 metres race at the Bislet Stadium in Oslo in 1957 from his fellow-countryman, Miroslav Jurek, and the Norwegians, Ernst Larsen (No. 166) and Öistein Saksvik. Jurek won in a track record of 14min 00.4sec and Zátopek finished a commendable 3rd, six seconds behind. By then his hairline, never that prominent, had receded even further.

Dana. Not just the supportive wife but a great champion in her own right who won Olympic gold in 1952 and European gold in 1954 and 1958. In fact, her career lasted longer than her husband's because she took part in every Olympic Games from 1948 to 1960 and she remained a World-class athlete for 17 years.

Among those most inspired by Zátopek's example were his fellow-countryman, Stanislav Jungwirth, and the Australian, Ron Clarke. Jungwirth, pictured above left beating Roger Bannister at 880 yards in 1954, set a World record at 1500 metres. Clarke broke 19 World records during his career, including this three miles, pictured below left, at the White City Stadium in 1965.

Human Locomotive'. Instead of accepting him as a challenge, many critics tried to explain him away as a freak. They said that at that pace he would burn up in a year. Yet, six years later Zátopek did his best ever performances and achieved World records in the 5000 and 10,000 metres.

"Zátopek upset British athletes because of the intensity of his training, his devotion and dedication, his amazing courage. He showed the critics, who were constantly telling young athletes to go easy for fear of killing themselves, that what they needed was more study, more and more training, and more and more discipline and courage. Not many were prepared to follow along that hard path. Since that day in 1948 there has been no place in my thoughts for anything that conflicted with my ideal, embodied in Zátopek".

In the early months of 1953 it seemed as if those critics of whom Pirie later wrote so scornfully might, regrettably, have been proved right. Zátopek was suffering from sciatica and found it painful to walk, much less run. He had his tonsils and some teeth removed. As had been the case the previous year he was nowhere near racing fitness when the season began. In March, at the International Cross-Country Championships, Franjo Mihalic had won on Yugoslavia's first appearance by 10 seconds from England's Frank Sando, and without prejudice to either of those two fine runners the more perceptive of the onlookers were again left wondering what Zátopek might have done, had he been there and in fine form.

In Moscow at the beginning of June a distance-running double was achieved of such a brilliance that only Zátopek could hitherto have contemplated it. On the first day of the match between Moscow, Leningrad and Kiev, Aleksandr Anufriyev ran a marvellous 5000 metres. He flew through the first kilometre in 2:39.0, and continuing on his own in his rather odd prancing style of running on his toes he went past 2000 metres in 5:24.0 and 3000 metres in 8:14.0 - which put him on target for 13:45! He was still three seconds up on Hägg's schedule at 4000 metres, but he was losing momentum and agonisingly missed the record by a fraction in 13:58.8. His successive kilometre "splits" of 2:39, 2:45, 2:50, 2:52 and 2:53 told the story. It had been a wonderful effort and totally unaided, with the next man, Vladimir Kuts, almost half-a-lap behind, though running a personal best of 14:28.8. The next day Anufriyev set a national record of 29:23.2 for 10,000 metres after passing halfway in 14:33. Only Zátopek had ever run faster.

Zátopek, by chance, had also run 14:33.0 in his first tentative 5000 metres of the year in May and had improved marginally to 14:26.8 on the same weekend as Anufriyev's double. At least Dana was in the best of spirits, breaking the national javelin record with a throw of 52.02m, but it didn't last. Her husband, in a not uncommon burst of high spirits, playfully threw her in a river while they were away for the weekend and she broke her ankle!

Against Hungary in Prague on 11-12 July he won convincingly at 5000 metres on the first day in 14:28.6 and at 10,000 on the second day in 29:48.6, a long way ahead of Jozsef Kovács. At the national championships at the Army's Strahov Stadium he won the 5000 metres on 24 July by a margin of 53 seconds in 14:11.4 and the 10,000 metres two days later in very hot weather by one and a half minutes in a modest 30:53.6. J. Armour Milne had expressed the belief that Zátopek was "in need of a lot of racing to get him into Olympic shape" and the old master was unobtrusively manoeuvring himself into form for what would be his major test of 1953 - the Communist Bloc "International World Youth Games" in Bucharest from 5-9 August. Anufriyev, for one, would be there.

The 5000 metres was held on the opening day in extremely hot weather. With Anufriyev, Zátopek, Kovács (who had run 14:07.4 the previous month) and Kuts (who had improved to 14:14.6) among the starters, it was a race of Olympian pretensions, and it was Kuts, a 26-year-old trained in a tough Soviet Marine school, who was the revelation. He led for the first two kilometres, and when Zátopek and Kovács caught him shortly afterwards he simply accelerated away again to a 30-metre lead. As Kozík described: "That was the situation two and a half laps from the finish, but by now we know a bit about Emil's fighting spirit when it comes to the decisive moments in a race. When it comes to it, he can always make a bigger sacrifice than the others. What was to be done? If he left the solution to the last few metres, he would not overtake Kuts. Kovács knew him and would be sure to be prepared for the last lap. There was only one other possibility, and that was to draw out the final struggle over two laps and start the finish 800 metres from the winning post".

It was yet another tactical twist to torment his rivals, and it worked. Zátopek caught Kuts in the home straight and won in 14:03.0, equalling his personal best from the 1950 European Championships. Kuts ran 14:04.0 to break his way dramatically into World class. Kovács was 3rd in 14:04.2. Anufriyev (as Gaston Meyer had surmised the year before) was maybe not the man for the big occasion and was 4th in 14:15.0. All four performances were faster than those of the runners who had occupied the same positions in the Olympic final in Helsinki.

The 10,000 metres took place on the final day of the meeting. Jungwirth, Skobla and the 200 metres runner, Václav Janecek, had all won their events for Czechoslovakia in the interim, and Jungwirth also took the 1500 metres on the last day. Only the USSR had been a more successful team than the Czechs. Zátopek faced Anufriyev and Kuts again, but it was entirely in character that Zátopek's schedule for the race was designed primarily to help a 24-year-old devotee of his methods who had travelled round the World to meet him. Dave Stephens had done nothing more of note than run 3000 metres in 8:29.0 in his native Australia the previous March but had got it into his head that he could break the national record for 5000 metres if he could meet up with the man he idolised.

Unfortunately, Stephens arrived in Bucharest too late for the 5000 metres race, but when he finally got to see Zátopek and told him what he wanted to do Zátopek asked him what the record was, and when he was informed that it was 14:35.0 and held by Les Perry (who was also, incidentally, a fanatical Zátopek copyist) simply arranged for Stephens to run the first 5000 metres of the 10,000. Zátopek also announced that he would set a 29:10 pace to ensure the intermediate time was fast enough for the record to be broken.

The Soviet runners set off at their usual hectic pace. Zátopek ignored them. Stephens dutifully followed in his master's footsteps and was then waved encouragingly ahead and duly went on to break the record with a time of 14:33.2. Zátopek had made yet another friend for life, and it did not really matter that the "record" which Stephens had beaten was not actually Les Perry's best. In Helsinki Perry had run much faster, but in myopic imitation of their British colleagues the Australian athletics authorities would only consider performances set on home soil. František Kozík clearly did not know about that aberration and therefore missed a prime opportunity for a bit of imperialist-bashing.

Zátopek, having performed wonders for Czechoslovak-Australian relations, reeled in the Reds in the second half of the race proper. Zátopek's winning time was 29:25.8, despite the searing heat, while Kuts was 2nd in 29:41.4 and Anufriyev well back 3rd in 30:03.4. It was another personal best for Kuts, and only Mimoun and Anufriyev had managed a faster time of all those who had finished in 2nd place in a race against Zátopek. Despite the margin of his victory Zátopek would have marked the new man down as one to watch. The two of them had apparently trained together during the week, which must have been an interesting session to watch. Zátopek v Kuts at 40 x 400 metres!

Zátopek, with other projects in mind, went back to his training track for some more intensive preparation, and even with his extensive knowledge of the capabilities and potential of all his peers he must have been surprised at the burst of activity that went on elsewhere in his absence. Gordon Pirie had broken the official World record for six miles with 28:19.4 at the AAA Championships in July, and even though Zátopek would have done about a quarter-of-a-minute faster if he had been timed in Turku three years before it was apparent that Pirie's achievement was still better in equivalent terms than anything which anybody except the Czech had ever done.

In rapid succession at the end of August and the beginning of September Zátopek slid several rungs down the rankings' ladder. At the Soviet championships in Moscow on 27 August Kuts ran 5000 metres in 14:02.2. At the Germany-v-GB match in Berlin two days later Pirie beat Schade by half-a-lap with 14:02.6. In Budapest on 20 September Kovács ran 14:01.2 to defeat Kuts in the Hungary-USSR meeting. At 10,000 metres Pirie formalised his 2nd place to Zátopek in the all-time reckoning with 29:17.2 against Sweden in Stockholm on 3 September.

On 17 October Zátopek asserted his authority, beating Kovács at 5000 metres in 14:09.0 on a windswept day at the Strahov Stadium. It was a superb contest, as J. Armour Milne recounted: "Kovács, having made Hungarian records recently for 5000 and 10,000 metres, was racing fit and ready to run the race of his life. He tackled Zátopek in the Czech's own style, returning sprint for sprint, repeatedly taking the lead and holding it, until with a lap to go Zátopek looked worn out as he dragged 20 yards or more in arrears. His chance of winning seemed hopeless at this point. Then out came the furious Zátopek finish. In less than a furlong he had wrapped up the 20 yards' deficit. Then he went racing on at breakneck speed to win by 25 yards or more".

Milne thought that the time would have been sub-14 on a decent day. It was damp and misty and the track was sodden, but Dana also enjoyed herself. Recovered from the ill-effects of Emil's boisterousness she reappeared in the 4 x 100 metres relay and the javelin.

Zátopek was clearly heartened by his form against Kovács, because it was apparently only after this race that he decided that something needed to be done about the fact that Pirie, Kovács and Anufriyev had all run faster 10,000 metres times than he had during the year. J. Armour Milne reported in "Athletics Weekly" that Zátopek was persuaded by his club officials to have "just one more try to improve your 10,000 metres time for the year". It was not until someone enterprisingly suggested that he should be timed at six miles en route that the thought occurred to Zátopek that if he was going to try for that record he might as well also go for the 10,000 record!

So much for structured State organisation and discipline! It was a typically improvised Zátopekian enterprise. His Army Club colleagues rallied together a field of 13 of Zátopek's disciples, inevitably including Jaroslav Šourek, to make it more of a show, and the chosen venue was again the salubrious Houštka Spa track in the Prague region of Bohemia. Zátopek, it seemed, was finely tuned to compose another Bohemian Rhapsody.

The overture was played by Josef Dolezal, the Olympic silver-medallist walker, who set out at 9.30 in the morning and broke the World records for 15,000 and 20,000 metres "walking easily and stylishly, not unlike Harry Churcher in action but with a longer step", according to the observant J. Armour Milne, recalling to mind for his "Athletics Weekly" readers a stalwart former British practitioner of the "heel and toe" art. Dolezal finished his 20 kilometres at just 26.4 seconds after 11 o'clock, and at 11.15 the conductor's baton was figuratively tapped once more, and Zátopek - in pursuit of his 29:02.6 from three years before - put on a marvellously judged display of metronomic running which was in complete contrast to the somewhat slapstick manner of his triple-record run at longer distances 12 months earlier.

He blithely ignored the fact that there was a chilly breeze, the atmosphere was damp, and the track was heavy - which is no more than one could expect if you chose, as Zátopek had perversely done, to try and run unprecedented times on such an inauspicious date as 1 November.

Zátopek 29:01.6, Houštka Spa, 1 November

2:52.8	2:55.8	2:55.2	2:55.8	2:55.2	2:53.8	2:55.4	2:55.6	2:57.2	2:44.8
	5:48.6	8:43.8	11:39.6	14:34.8	17:28.6	20:24.0	23:19.6	26:16.8	29:01.6

He had beaten his record by just one second, and it was almost possible to believe that he had engineered the time to ensure that he still had another interesting target to aim for in the future. He had kept a couple of seconds or so inside his 1950 "split" times through to 6000 metres, stayed level until 8000 metres, lost a couple of seconds in the ninth kilometre, but then produced a barnstorming finish. His last kilometre was by far the fastest ever run in a World record race, and only he had ever previously got within five seconds of it. He passed six miles in 28:08.4 to relieve Pirie of that record, and Pirie himself would not have been in the least surprised. He knew that he had held the record only on temporary loan.

The oft-forgotten "also rans" in Zátopek's record-breaking spree all performed very creditably. By no means overawed, they staged a spirited race of their own the best part of two laps behind: Milos Tomis ran 31:12.2, Jaroslav Liska 31:12.4, Jaroslav Šourek 31:20.0, Miroslav Hercik 31:22.6 and Ivan Ullsperger 31:35.6. All were personal bests, and Tomis ranked 69th in the World for the year, Liska 70th, Šourek 80th, and Hercik and Ullsperger in the top 100. That was twice as many as Czechoslovakia had provided in 1952, and that would have appealed to Zátopek's good nature almost as much as the thought that he was still beyond doubt the World's best distance runner.

MORE WORLD RECORDS IN 1952 AND 1953

WORLD'S ALL-TIME BEST AT 5,000 METRES

At the end of 1953:

13:58.2	Gunder Hägg (Sweden)	(1)	Gothenburg (WR)	20.09.42
13:58.8	Aleksandr Anufriyev (USSR)	(1)	Moscow	06.06.53
14:01.2	Jozsef Kovács (Hungary)	(1)	Budapest	20.09.53
14:02.2	Vladimir Kuts (USSR)	(1)	Moscow	27.08.53
14:02.6	Gordon Pirie (GB)	(1)	Berlin	29.08.53
14:03.0	Emil Zátopek (Czecho)	(1)	Brussels	26.08.50
14:06.6	Herbert Schade (Germany)	(1)	Stuttgart	08.06.52
14:07.4	Alain Mimoun (France)	(2)	Helsinki (OG)	24.07.52
14:08.6	Sydney Wooderson (GB)	(1)	Oslo (E Ch)	23.08.46
14:08.8	Taisto Mäki (Finland)	(1)	Helsinki (WR)	16.06.39
14:08.8	Vladimir Kazantsev (USSR)	(1)	Leningrad	02.07.52

Note: Zátopek had equalled his best of 14:03.0 in 1953.

WORLD'S ALL-TIME BEST AT 10,000 METRES

At the end of 1953:

29:01.6	Emil Zátopek (Czecho)	(1)	Stará Boleslav	01.11.53
29:17.2	Gordon Pirie (GB)	(1)	Stockholm	03.09.53
29:21.2	Jozsef Kovács (Hungary)	(1)	Bucharest	04.10.53
29:23.2	Aleksandr Anufriyev (USSR)	(1)	Moscow	07.06.53
29:23.8	Valter Nyström (Sweden)	(1)	Düsseldorf	14.09.52
29:24.8	Herbert Schade (Germany)	(2)	Düsseldorf	14.09.52
29:27.2	Viljo Heino (Finland)	(1)	Kouvola	01.09.49
29:29.4	Alain Mimoun (France)	(1)	Stockholm	04 10.52
29:41.4	Vladimir Kuts (USSR)	(2)	Bucharest	09.08.53
29:46.0	Bertil Albertsson (Sweden)	(1)	Uppsala	14.10.51

10.

TWO WORLD RECORDS IN THREE DAYS IN 1954

"Why shouldn't the World record-holder one day be called Pirie?"

IT WAS A TIME FOR philosophical reflection. Emil Zátopek, despite his new record at 10,000 metres, was far from complacent. J. Armour Milne, Zátopek's faithful but forthright scribe, could read the signs.

"Why shouldn't the World record-holder at 10,000 metres one day be called Pirie?", Zátopek realistically observed at the end of 1953. "Whoever surpasses my training will also break my records, as long as he doesn't burn himself out too soon. Pirie is still very very young and at his age one shouldn't force the longer distances too much. Pirie is also, of course, extremely good over the shorter distances, but if he wants to achieve something really exceptional over the longer distances he must become still better over the shorter distances".

Zátopek, generous as always, had further good advice to offer his Soviet rivals, Anufriyev and Kuts: "These two also have it in them to beat my records. Both have tremendously strong constitutions and are young and eager. The one thing wrong with them, in my opinion, is their tactics. They set off every time at such a pace as if they are going to break the World record by half-a-minute. If they would just hold themselves back a bit, then my times would be broken. Yet I don't think they will".

Regarding his own capabilities, Zátopek's mood was sombre for once. "You must not expect too much from me in the future. You must get used to the fact - and I must be content with it - that I shall be able to compete in the shorter of the long distances only as a sort of 'guest artist'. I feel that my true distances are from 10,000 metres upwards. There I could still achieve so much".

Zátopek would have been well aware of Pirie's range of talents. He would have known that he had beaten Wes Santee, the USA's voluble sub-four-minute candidate, in a 4:06.8 mile, and that was quicker than Zátopek had ever aspired to, and probably half a dozen seconds better than he could now achieve. At 3000 metres there did not appear, at least on paper, to be much difference. Kuts had done 8:10.4, Pirie 8:11.0 and Zátopek a gratifying 8:13.8 during the year, but Kuts's time had been achieved in a 5000 metres race and Pirie's only two days after his fastest 10,000 metres.

Reviewing the year, J. Armour Milne had these words of warning to impart, even concerning the 10,000 metres: "Zátopek's initial speed is receding rather than improving with the passing of time. The new Soviet star, Kuts, showed this in Bucharest. He also demonstrated a possible way of beating the triple Olympic champion, and where he failed Pirie with his superior miling pace might succeed. Kuts got away from Zátopek early on, and it took everything that Zátopek had to bring the Soviet runner back to him.

"The secret of Zátopek's success has been his ability to get to the front after about two laps, and once there to wear the opposition down by the application of bursts of speed at irregular intervals. Against Kuts this failed to work. Kuts raced quickly into a lead, then ran smoothly, undisturbed by challenging sprints until Zátopek got him near the end. If someone like Pirie can repeat the performance he may have enough speed to get so far ahead that Zátopek won't be able to get near enough to make use of his famous finishing burst".

Yet in the same year that Milne, such a prolific and perceptive chronicler, was bemoaning Zátopek's lack of speed, others were expressing a startlingly contrasting view. Zátopek himself made mention of a time of 3min 45sec for 1500 metres, giving the distinct impression that he believed he was capable of that, while authoritative opinions were expressed in Britain - where there was such a host of admirers - to the effect that he could do better still. Throughout 1953 and in the early months of 1954 speculation was feverish as to who would be the first man to break four minutes for the mile, with Roger Bannister (Great Britain), John Landy (Australia) and Wes Santee (USA) all running 4:02.0, or very close to it, and regarded as the prime contenders. The names of a number of others were bandied about as outsiders, including those of Gordon Pirie, Gaston Reiff ... and Zátopek.

No less an expert observer than Harold Abrahams, the Olympic 100 metres gold-medallist from 1924, who had become one of the sport's foremost administrators and journalists, came up with this most radical suggestion regarding who could break the "four-minute barrier". Writing in the January 1953 issue of "World Sports", the official magazine of the British Olympic Association, Abrahams listed most of the obvious four-minute candidates and then added, almost as if it was an afterthought, "I am not at all sure that Emil Zátopek would not have something to say about the 4-minute mile if he was minded so to do". By way of explanation, Abrahams concluded: "Maybe I'm over-susceptible to Emil's fantastic powers, but a man who can run the last 400 metres of a 5000 metres race in well inside a minute cannot be ruled out as a possibility for a 4-minute mile".

Later that year Abrahams's claim was endorsed by the McWhirter twins, who knew more about international athletics than anyone else in Britain at the time. Taking up the soothsayer's challenge in their monthly magazine, "Athletics World", they concluded that so far as breaking four minutes was concerned "the real man for the job, though perhaps he doesn't know it, is Emil Zátopek". As Zátopek had never run a mile race in his life, and his best 1500 metres of 3:52.8 dated from six years previously and was worth no more than 4:11 for the classic distance, all this conjecture could have been dismissed as being entirely fanciful, but neither the erudite Abrahams, who had trained in the law, nor the McWhirters, who shared in equal measure the virtues of passion for the sport and preciseness in their observations about it, were given to making hasty judgments.

There is absolutely no evidence whatsoever that Zátopek ever gave thought to the mile. Had he done so, he would surely have changed his mind after Bannister ran his historic 3:59.4 in May of 1954. In any case, Emil came up with the perfect riposte. Within a month he was to do yet again what he did best, and that was to set new World records at 5000 and 10,000 metres. Nevertheless, it remains an intriguing thought. His reckoning that he could run 3:45 for 1500 metres was worth 4:03 for the mile, and that was only a second or less slower than the elite specialists were achieving. Perhaps as early as 1948, when he ran 8:07.8 for 3000 metres, he could have shown himself capable of threatening the then World record for the mile of 4:01.3, set by the Swede, Gunder Hägg, in 1945. Perhaps.

At the end of 1953 Zátopek was given permission by the Czech authorities to accept an invitation for the Sao Paulo New Year's Eve road race in Brazil. From the moment of his arrival it was a bizarre experience. He was met by hordes of pressmen and hundreds of well-wishers when his plane landed at the airport. Radio and television interviewers besieged his hotel room. When he and the Austrian competitor, Adolf Gruber, decided to go out for an exploratory training run along the course they were escorted by police motorcyclists and pursued by a frenzied convoy of cameramen. Zátopek, being Zátopek, enjoyed the attention hugely.

The Sao Paulo event had started in 1924 with 60 competitors. For the 1953 race there were 2,140 from 16 different nations. Viljo Heino had won in 1949, and the Yugoslav, Franjo Mihalic, who had set a course record of 21min 28sec the previous year, was taking part again. Others with whom Zátopek was familiar were Theys, of Belgium, and Taipale, of Finland. Though only 7,300 metres in length, it was, and it remains, one of the most demanding events imaginable, starting at 11.45 p.m. in oppressively sultry heat, with many of the local competitors setting off smartly before the official signal, and a million or more spectators in festive mood scarcely held in check along the steeply undulating city streets.

Zátopek revelled in it. Within 500 metres he had caught the tearaways, and the other 2,139 runners never saw him again. He won in a new record of 20min 30sec, with Mihalic just outside his previous record but more than a minute behind. The McWhirters, writing in "Athletics World", worked it out that even at level pace on the oft-measured course Zátopek would have gone through 5000 metres in 14:02.4!

To prove - as if it needed proving - that he was capable of running a World-class 10,000 metres anywhere, against anyone, and at any time of the year, Zátopek then won a track race at that distance in front of 20,000 spectators in Sao Paulo a week later. It had rained continuously for the previous three days, but Zátopek (probably thinking to himself 'This is just like Houštka Spa') toured comfortably round in 30:09.0. Just as was customary in Houštka Spa, the next finisher in Sao Paulo came in two laps later.

Only a dozen men had run better than 30:09.0 in 1953, so Zátopek was already setting a hot pace a few days into the New Year, buoyed in the knowledge that Berne and the European titles he was to defend in seven months' time formed the serious objective. Having looked at the Championships timetable and seen that both the 10,000 metres and the marathon were on the opening day, he had opted for the two track events. No suggestion was ever made that maybe the World's most famous athlete could be accommodated by switching the marathon to the final day, and nor would Zátopek have expected it.

Zátopek's next visit of note was to Paris for the annual cross-country races organised by the Communist newspaper, "*L'Humanité*", to which the leading Eastern Bloc athletes were invited. The French Federation - in a fit of pique because the entries had been sent direct to the promoters and not to them - refused permission for him and others to run. They raced, anyway, in a hastily arranged "unofficial" 10km event and Zátopek won as he liked in 30:34. Jerzy Chromik, of Poland, finished next 52 seconds behind, and he was still ahead of Kuts, Pozhidayev and Anufriyev for the Soviet Union.

After a winter of heavier training than ever before, the opening of Zátopek's track season was nothing short of sensational. During a training camp for European Championships contenders he ran a 5000 metres race at Houštka Spa on 14 May. His successive kilometres were 2:47.6, 2:50.8, 2:49.4, 2:51.4 and 2:44.8 for a concluding time of 14:04.0. He had never begun a season in such style, and his previous fastest debut 5000 for the year had been 14:08.2 back in 1947. Could it be that the wise old joker had been deliberately leading people astray with all his talk of being no more than a "guest artist" these days at 5000 metres? This was "Top Of The Bill" stuff, and no doubt about it.

J. Armour Milne had reported that Zátopek had put in more kilometres than ever during the winter and that "at long last his training methods had been vindicated at home, where they have been confined largely to Zátopek himself". A school of "Zátopekovites" had been formed, all of its pupils training along Zátopek lines, and the Houštka Spa race presented the exam results for all to see: Ivan Ullsperger 14:33.6 (improving 24.4sec), Miroslav Koubek 14:35.8 (improving 11.4sec), Milos Tomis 14:36.4 (improving 11.2sec), Jaroslav Slavicek 14:37.0 (improving 32.4sec).

Zátopek went off to Paris and Brussels for races at 5000 metres and then 10,000 metres on Sunday 30 May and Tuesday 1 June. It certainly was not a matter of seeking opposition because there wasn't any of real stature, and presumably the mini-tour was a matter of some sort of political correctness. There was certainly no talk beforehand of record attempts, though he was obviously in exceptional form. At Stade Colombes on Sunday evening he was faced only with four others, and the best of them was Stritof, the No.2 Yugoslav to Mihalic whose solitary record-breaking performance had been a share in the national best at 4 x 1500 metres four years before. Much the most reputable of the assorted Belgians lining up in the out-of-the-way Stade Trois Tillauts on Tuesday night was Marcel van de Wattyne, who had at least come 10th in the recent Zátopek-less International Cross-Country Championships, though a long way behind the winner, Alain Mimoun.

In Paris every one of Zátopek's kilometre "splits" was faster than in his 14:04.0 earlier in the month. On his own after 300 metres, he charged through successive stages in 2:47.2, 2:47.2 again, 2:49.0 and 2:50.0 and then caught up all that had been lost to Gunder Hägg's schedule, and more besides, with a superlative last kilometre of 2:43.8 and a finishing time of 13:57.2! Yet, as R.L. Quercetani so rightly pointed out in his report for "Athletics World", "the echo of Bannister's Dream Mile was still audible". Roger Bannister had earned Worldwide acclaim with the first sub-four-minute mile earlier in May and the value of Zátopek's achievement was perhaps not properly appreciated.

His separate lap times had been mesmeric: 66.8, 66.7, 66.6, 66.9, 67.4, 67.4, 65.8, 69.8 (a touch of familiar eccentricity here), 66.4, 69.6, 69.0 and then 1:34.8 for the last 600 metres. Drago Stritof was 2nd in 14:42.3, and the experience did him no harm because he improved to

14:23.8 and 30th ranking in the World before the summer was out. Unfortunately, no immediate time was taken at three miles, at which point Zátopek might well have been faster than Hagg's official record of 13:32.4. It was not the only occasion on which Zátopek was deprived of a record in such a way.

"The 5000 metres race, with that amazing last kilometre of 2:43.8, confirms that Zátopek is still the master as regards pace judgment and finishing speed", concluded Dr Quercetani. "Even more enlightening, perhaps, are the considerations suggested by his 10,000 metres two days later. On this occasion Zátopek ran the first half in 14:27.6, the second in 14:26.6. So it can be said that he BEAT PAAVO NURMI'S BEST FOR 5000 METRES (14:28.2) TWICE ON END (RLQ's capital letters). In more English terms, Zátopek is the first man to run the equivalent of <u>two consecutive three miles</u> (RLQ's underlining) in less than 14 minutes apiece!"

Zátopek 13:57.2, Paris, 30 May 1954

2:47.1	2:47.2	2:49.0	2:50.0	2:43.8
	5:34.4	8:23.4	11:13.4	13:57.2

Zátopek's time of 28:54.2 in Brussels broke way through the 29-minute barrier he had perhaps purposely left unbreached the year before. On the way he also beat 28 minutes for six miles with his official time of 27:59.2. Once he had established by halfway an advantage of seven seconds or so over his intermediate times of the previous year he maintained his margin of comfort with absolute precision. It was his 14th World record in nine different events. Only Hannes Kolehmainen, with his 14:36.6/31:20.8 double at the 1912 Olympics had set two such World records within three days.

Zátopek 28:54.2, Brussels, 1 June, 1954

2:47.8	2:56.4	2:54.0	2:55.8	2:53.6	2:55.4	2:53.4	2:55.2	2:55.8	2:46.8
	5:44.2	8:38.2	11:34.0	14:27.6	17:23.0	20:16.4	23:11.6	26:07.4	28:54.2

No one else was in remotely comparable form, though the following weekend Chris Chataway ran the second fastest ever two miles in 8:41.0, beating Zátopek's compatriot, Stanislav Jungwirth, in the British Games at the White City. The Czech sprinter, Václav Janecek, was also taking part in the meeting and it seems a pity that Zátopek could not have been invited to come on to London from Brussels. The meeting schedule would have had to be rearranged because the other distance events more suited to the week's World record-breaker were the Inter-Counties' three miles (won by Gordon Pirie) and six miles (won by Frank Sando). The three miles would have been an interesting spectacle had Zátopek been there in his self-appointed role as "guest artist" because Pirie ran the first mile at 13:06 pace, compared with Hägg's still surviving record of 13:32.4!

Instead, Zátopek raced just once more in June, winning a 5000 metres in Prague in 14:17.8, and concentrated on his mammoth training sessions instead. The Hungary-v-Czechoslovakia match took place in Budapest on 3-4 July, with Zátopek meeting Jozsef Kovács at 10,000 metres on the first day. Kovács had run a 30:04.0 at the beginning of June and Zátopek, not unreasonably, had thought that 29:35 would be enough to win and went through the first half almost exactly as planned in 14:48, but the remainder of the race was in an altogether different league. Successive kilometres were run in 2:53, 2:57, 2:55 and 2:54 as the red-vested Zátopek and his slighter opponent in all white fought it out shoulder-to-shoulder. Kovács led with 800 metres to go; Zátopek led with 200 metres to go; but with a last lap of 59.2 it was the Hungarian who got away to win by five metres. Kovács ran the second fastest time ever of 29:09.0. Zátopek ran 29:09.8 and it was the first occasion on which he had been beaten at the distance in 38 races since his debut in 1948.

It was a victory of the utmost significance by Kovács because it served to herald the upsurge of Hungarian distance running which would sweep away so many World records the following year. For Zátopek, it was probably not as disappointing as one might have supposed. It was said later that he was not in full health that day, and in any case he probably reasoned that a defeat even at 10,000 metres would have to happen sometime, and better for it not to happen when a gold medal was at stake. He had said before that Kovács would beat him if he was still with him in the last lap. In Berne Zátopek would now be more intent than ever on having the last lap to himself.

ZÁ-TO-PEK! ZÁ-TO-PEK! ZÁ-TO-PEK!

The next day Zátopek just beat Miklós Szábo at 5000 metres, but J. Armour Milne certainly took a phlegmatic view of the Budapest results: "Zátopek's first defeat over 10,000 metres naturally shook the athletics world, but I advise sanity in weighing it up. One defeat doesn't mean the end of the great Zátopek. Emil realises that he had himself to blame for his defeat, and despite his World records at 5000 and 10,000 metres it is clear that he still does not have the speed in his limbs that permits of an athlete running a waiting race. Now he must go back to his old tactics of wearing the opposition down by his unorthodox and repeated bursts of speed".

At the AAA Championships the next weekend Freddie Green and Chris Chataway jointly edged two-tenths inside Hägg's World record for three miles, which had lasted for 12 years. Pirie, suffering a persistent foot injury, did not run and now seemed out of the reckoning for the season. Vladimir Kuts had begun his year with 5000 metres times of 14:12.8 and 14:11.6. Zátopek was so dissatisfied with his 5000 metres win in 14:24.8 on the first day of the Czech championships that he did not contest the 10,000 two days later, and he now believed that he had trained too hard during the winter and had reached his peak too soon. Was this really so? Or was this Emil talking himself down again? The European Championships would begin in less than three weeks' time on 25 August.

11.

EUROPEAN CHAMPIONSHIPS AGAIN IN 1954

The Marine outflanks the Colonel on his own favourite battle ground

THE 23 RUNNERS gathering on the damp and clinging cinders of the Neufeld Stadium in Berne shortly before 7.15 on the evening of Wednesday 25 August at the 1954 European Championships represented the finest assembly of 10,000-metre expertise ever seen. When the Helsinki Olympic race had been held two years previously there had been five men who had beaten 30 minutes. In Berne there were twice that number who had done that or the equivalent at six miles. Four of the six fastest ever were there. The only obvious absentees were Kuts, concentrating on the 5000, and the injury-struck Pirie and Mimoun.

The leading contenders were Zátopek (Czechoslovakia) 28:54.2, Kovács (Hungary) 29:09.0, Anufriyev (USSR) 29:23.4, Schade (Germany) 29:24.8, Mihalic (Yugoslavia) 29:37.6, Basalayev (USSR) 29:45.4, Posti (Finland) 29:49.8, Saksvik (Norway) 29:50.6, Sando (GB) 29:51.8, Ozog (Poland) 30:01.4, Juhász (Hungary) 30:02.2, Miecznikowski (Poland) 30:07.0, Nilsson (Sweden) 30:09.6, Theys (Belgium) 30:16.6. At six miles - Driver (GB) 28:34.8. Not far off the list was one of the " Zátopekovites", Jiri Šantrucek, who had won the Czech national title in the absence of his guru in a commendable 30:22.6.

It was Zátopek's eighth track final in major Championships. He had won the 1948 Olympic Games 10,000 metres by 47.8 seconds, the 1950

ZÁ-TO-PEK! ZÁ-TO-PEK! ZÁ-TO-PEK!

European Championships 10,000 metres by one minute and nine seconds, and the 1952 Olympic Games 10,000 metres by 15.8 seconds. There seemed every likelihood that even after his recent World record the margin would be a narrow one this time. Zátopek thrilled to the challenge, as the very first words of the description of the race by the McWhirters in the September 1954 issue of "Athletics World" bear immediate evidence:

"This was perhaps Zátopek's greatest run ever. The track was heavy with the rain of the five previous days and the temperature one which even the Finns declared to be well below the ideal. The Colonel ran, however, to within less than four seconds of his 86-day-old World record.

"Contrary to his usual practice, the 31-year-old Czech went straight into the lead from the three-tier start to complete the first lap in 68.8sec. Only Herbert Schade, of Germany, tried to hang on to his agonising pace and paid the price with a 4th place. Both the tiny Hungarian, Kovács, and Britain's 23-year-old Frank Sando wisely ran for high placings. With 10 of the 25 laps gone, Zátopek had ground himself nearly 50 yards clear of Schade, with Kovács 3rd, Sando 4th and the tall 1953 International Cross-Country champion, Franjo Mihalic, 5th, and Peter Driver, the Empire champion, 10th.

"At the halfway mark reached in 14:28.0 Zátopek was nearly 100 metres ahead of Schade, who was himself 30 metres ahead of Sando and Kovács, with Driver now 9th. Though drawing steadily away, Zátopek's pace was very slightly dropping, since the last half occupied 14:30.0. In the 22nd lap Sando and Kovács went past Schade, and attention switched to their private duel in the same way as it did four days later with Chataway and the brilliant Czech. The Hungarian, galvanised by the bell, shot past Sando with a 64.8sec last lap.

"Out ahead Zátopek, possessed by all the demons in hell, was killing himself in trying to lap Peter Driver before the exploding flash bulbs gave the signal that he could now go over and congratulate his wife on winning the women's javelin with a new championship best performance. Of the next five to finish only Sando, who received quite an ovation on the victory stand, recorded a personal best".

EUROPEAN CHAMPIONSHIPS AGAIN IN 1954

Zátopek 28:58.0, Berne, 25 August - His 400 metres lap times:

68.8	70.8	69.1	68.1	69.0	69.1	68.7	68.6	69.8
69.9	69.9	70.6	70.4	70.0	69.4	70.6	71.0	70.8
70.4	69.6	71.3	69.1	71.3	68.9	63.0		

His other recorded intermediate times of note were 800m 2:19.6, 2000m 5:45.6, 3000m 8:37.4, 4000m 11:31.7, 3 miles 13:57.2, 5000m 14:28.0, 6000m 17:22.0, 8000m 23:14.4, 9000m 26:10.5, 6 miles 28:03.5. His margin of victory on this occasion was 27.8sec.

The 5000 metres heats the following day were completed with no great drama, though Zátopek managed to make something of a comedy out of his, jogging in with the Finn, Julin, for the remaining qualifying places and totally unaware that the Swiss runner, Pierre Page, was bearing down on them at great speed. Zátopek, in the words of the McWhirters, "clapped his hands to his mouth like a naughty boy whose stone had just missed the vicarage greenhouse" when he realised it had been such a close-run thing. Page, like the Dane, Planck, in Zátopek's Helsinki Olympic heat, was rewarded with a national record for his temerity. There was another national record for Portugal in the third heat - long before the days of World-class athletes such as Mamede, Lopes and Leitão, it was a mere 14:55.8.

The final was held at 4.25 on the afternoon of Sunday 29 August and the 15 qualifiers, with their best times, were Zátopek (Czechoslovakia) 13:57.2, Kovács (Hungary) 14:01.2, Kuts (USSR) 14:02.2, Schade (Germany) 14:06.6, Hanswijck (Belgium) 14:11.0, Garay (Hungary) 14:13.4, Haikkola (Finland) 14:14.2, Julin (Finland) 14:15.0, Okorokov (USSR) 14:16.0, Graj (Poland) 14:16.8, Herman (Belgium) 14:18.0, Saksvik (Norway) 14:19.2, Laufer (Germany) 14:28.4. At three miles - Green (GB), Chataway (GB) both 13:32.2. At the 1952 Olympics there had only been four finalists who had previously run sub-14:20. In Berne all but one of the 15 had done so, or run the equivalent at three miles.

The race was expected to be between Zátopek, Kovács, Kuts and Chataway, and again the McWhirters provided the definitive report of the contest:

"No man ever more effectively ruined a race than did the fair-haired Russian. With head slightly back and eyes almost heavenward, he lumbered off lap after lap with his lead growing at every heavy tread. In the wake of this fabulous running the rest of the field was hopelessly demoralised. Laufer and Green retired, as did both Kovács and Schade. It was noteworthy that the only man to approach remotely his personal best was the other Russian, Vladimir Okorokov, whose 4th place was only four seconds outside his previous best.

"Kuts sliced 4.4sec off Green and Chataway's 50-day-old World record for three miles during his 65.6sec last lap with 13:27.6, later corrected to 13:27.8. The dispossessed holder, Chris Chataway, well knew after four or five laps that the Russian had escaped, but it was not his day, and he was only too thankful that Zátopek, too, was not in top shape. Nonetheless, the 23-year-old Englishman had to find a sapping last lap of 59.3sec to quell the ever game Czech, whose bronze medal will look singularly out of place in the private bullion horde which he and Dana have accumulated in the past six years".

Kuts ran successive kilometres of 2:44.0, 2:52.7, 2:47.2 (3000m in 8:23.9), 2:48.4 and 2:44.3 for a new World record of 13:56.6. The damage to his opponents and to Zátopek's record had been done in the third and fourth kilometre stages; together, they were 3.4sec faster than Zátopek had run in Paris. The McWhirters gave a pen-picture of Kuts which revealed that he had been a Marine since the age of 17 and had originally been a boxer, rower and skier and had only taken up running in 1951 at 24. His first performance of note had been 6th place in the 1952 USSR championships in 14:56.0. He had improved to 14:32.2 that year and to 14:02.2 in 1953. The month before the European Championships he had run the third fastest ever 3000 metres in 8:05.8.

10,000 metres: 1 Zátopek (Czechoslovakia) 28:58.0, 2 Kovács (Hungary) 29:25.8, 3 Sando (GB) 29:27.6; 4 Schade (Germany) 29:32.8, 5 Mihalic (Yugoslavia) 29:59.6, 6 Driver (GB) 30:03.6, 7 Saksvik (Norway) 30:04.4, 8 Anufriyev (USSR) 30:19.4, 9 Nilsson (Sweden) 30:22.4, 10 Vuchkov (Bulgaria) 30:25.2 (national record), 11 Schudel (Switzerland) 30:26.4 (national record); 12 Basalayev (USSR) 30:29.4, 13 Ozog (Poland) 30:37.2, 14 Posti (Finland) 30:39.4, 15 Thögersen (Denmark) 30:53.4; 16 Silva (Portugal) 30:59.0 (national record), 17

Morgenthaler (Switzerland) 31:10.4, 18 Šantrucek (Czechoslovakia) 31:11.2, 19 Theys (Belgium) 31:26.6, 20 Ozcan (Turkey) 31:42.4, 21 Amorós (Spain) 31:50.8. Did not finish - Juhász (Hungary), Miecznikowski (Poland).

5000 metres: 1 Kuts (USSR) 13:56.6, 2 Chataway (GB) 14:08.8, 3 Zátopek (Czechoslovakia) 14:10.2, 4 Okorokov (USSR) 14:20.0, 5 Hanswijck (Belgium) 14:25.6, 6 Herman (Belgium) 14:31.4, 7 Saksvik (Norway) 14:32.2, 8 Julin (Finland) 14:32.4, 9 Garay (Hungary) 14:44.6, 10 Graj (Poland) 14:48.6, 11 Haikkola (Finland) 15:22.8. Did not finish - Green (GB), Kovács (Hungary), Laufer (Germany), Schade (Germany).

Zátopek was clearly determined to make some sort of riposte at the shorter distance because in Stockholm only four days later he almost got his record back again! With no one to help him, he started much faster than he ever had before - 2:43, 2:47 and 2:49 for 8:19.0 at 3000m - but the record hopes slipped away with a 2:52 for the next kilometre and Zátopek simply did not have the speed in his legs to cut the mere half-second off his final kilometre which would have sufficed to overtake Kuts. The final time was 13:57.0.

On reflection Zátopek had every reason to be well satisfied with his showing all-round in Berne. He had won the 10,000 in the fastest time ever in a major Championships. Kuts had run only the 5000, and taken his chance well, and when he won the 10,000 at the USSR championships in Kiev on 12 September his time, though a national record 29:21.4, was still not quite of Zátopek vintage. Kovács and Schade, who had both also tried the double in Berne, had not lasted the course in the 5000, and the only other one who had done so was the Norwegian, Saksvik, with two 7th places.

There was actually another Czech athlete who performed an intrinsically better Berne double than Zátopek, and that was the walker, Josef Dolezal, who won the 10,000 metres track event and then came 2nd in the 50 kilometres on the road, and even he had declared that he was adopting Zátopek's training policies. It was altogether a good Championships for Mr and Mrs Zátopek's team-mates, as they also took bronze medals for Martin Rehak in the triple jump, Olga Modrachová in the high jump and Stanislav Jungwirth at 1500 metres.

Jungwirth presumptuously beat one of Zátopek's national records with 8:05.4 for 3000 metres at the end of October, but by then Zátopek had weightier matters to ponder. Chataway had defeated Kuts, 13:51.6 to 13:51.7, in an unforgettable 5000 metres race during the London-v-Moscow match under floodlights on 13 October, and for those of us who were there that night it was scarcely credible that Kuts was able to run a shade faster at the Strahov Stadium in Prague 10 days later.

Not only had Kuts beaten the record on Zátopek's own territory but he had beaten Zátopek himself by a massive margin on the first day of the Czechoslovakia-USSR match in front of a crowd of 50,000. Kuts followed the same tactics as in Berne and after his first lap in 59.4 had a lead of 40 metres which continued to grow for the rest of the race. He ran 2:38.4, 2:52.4 and 2:51.8 for each of the first three kilometres (8:22.6 at 3000m), then added 2:45.0 and 2:43.6, and despite a last lap eight seconds slower than in the monumental battle with Chataway he marginally improved the record to 13:51.2.

Zátopek ran arguably the worst major 5000 of his career in 14:19.0. It was his first defeat in a significant race in his own country since 1948. Yet, unabashed, he ran the opening half of the next day's 10,000 metres in 14:29 and convinced the crowd and officials for a while that he might even challenge his own World record. He was "struggling badly all the way through the second half", according to J. Armour Milne's report for "Athletics Weekly", but he still beat Anufriyev by almost a minute.

Milne felt bound to pose the rhetorical question, "Is Zátopek on the way out?", and in response suggested that "the obvious explanation of Zátopek's in-and-out form this year is that even the Czech iron man hasn't been able to stand up to the nightmare training programme he set himself from the beginning of last winter. Otherwise, not even Kuts would have beaten him by 175 yards in 5000 metres. It has been a bitter lesson for the Olympic champion, but at least he is capable of appreciating the situation".

EUROPEAN CHAMPIONSHIPS AGAIN IN 1954

How the World record-breaking 5000 metres races compared

	1000m	2000m	3000m	4000m	3 miles	Last km
Hägg, Gothenburg 1942	13:58.2	2:40.0	5:27.0	8:18.5	11:09.0	13:32.4	2:49.2
Zátopek, Paris 1954	13:57.2	2:47.2	5:34.4	8:23.4	11:13.4	n.t.	2:43.8
Kuts, Berne 1954	13:56.6	2:44.0	5:36.7	8:23.9	11:12.2	13:27.8	2:44.4
Chataway, London 1954	13:51.6	2:41.6	5:31.7	8:16.8	11:10.0	13:27.1	2:41.6
Kuts, Prague 1954	13:51.2	2:38.5	5:30.8	8:22.6	11:07.6	13:26.4	2:43.7
AT LEVEL PACE	13:51.2	2:46.2	5:32.5	8:18.7	11:04.9	13:22.6	2:46.2

The 5000 metres record which had lasted 12 years had now improved seven seconds in less than five months. The fastest of each kilometre stages gave an aggregate of 13:37.0, though it would presumably need somebody with the speed of Hägg, the spirit of Chataway, the stamina of Kuts - and, above all, the single-mindedness of Zátopek - to do it. The most likely candidate remained a man who ranked equal 13th in the World at 1500 metres in 1954 and did not figure at all at 5000 metres, though his brother did. In late October Gordon Pirie, who had taken a job as a paint salesman earlier in the year, had reappeared after injury and beaten Anufriyev at three miles on a cold and wet night in Manchester.

The 5000 metres rankings had taken something of a battering during the year. The 10th best performer of the year had run 14:14.2, compared with 14:16.0 in 1952, The 25th best performers were, respectively, 14:21.2 and 14:23.6. The 50th best were 14:30.4 and 14:37.2. Taking the event in isolation, it was still to all intents and purposes a European preserve, because of the top 100 only two - Warren, of Australia (37th), and Takahashi, of Japan (83rd) - were from outside the old continent. Finland, oddly, led with 13 athletes in the list, followed by Hungary and USSR with 12 each; Great Britain 10; Germany and Sweden nine each; Czechoslovakia six; France, Norway and Poland five each; Yugoslavia four; Belgium three; Turkey two; Australia, Austria, Japan, Spain and Switzerland one each. The Australian, Geoff Warren, was another dedicated Zátopek imitator, to whom Les Perry had passed on the shirt and shorts given to him by Zátopek in Helsinki.

Apart from Finland's apparent renaissance - which could probably be attributed to the fact that they simply held a lot of 5000-metre races - the most significant advances were those of Hungary, Great Britain and Czechoslovakia. The Hungarians, inspired by the coaching of Mihály Igloí, actually had five of the first 17 places with Kovács, Iharos, Garay,

103

Szabó and Béres. Britain's qualifiers were Chataway, Ken Norris, Maynard, <u>Peter</u> Pirie, Pemble, Driver, Foord, Perkins, Disley and Green. The five other Czechs were Ullsperger (33rd at 14:25.2), Šantrucek, Koubek, Tomis and Slavicek. A truer picture, though, is provided if the three miles rankings are also taken into account.

It needs to be pointed out that in the 1950s, and for that matter for most of the 1960s, the British Empire & Commonwealth nations persisted with the imperial measure, and many athletes in Britain, Australia and New Zealand never ran metric events at all. In 1954 there were 36 runners who were listed in the "World Sports International Athletics Annual" at faster than 14:10.0 for three-mile races, and if those who were not already named at 5000 metres are included in the combined rankings for the two distances then Great Britain's tally rises to 29! Among the more notable additions are Sando, Gordon Pirie, Fred Norris, Ken Wood and Derek Ibbotson.

A detailed survey in the January 1955 issue of "Athletics World" showed how the balance of power had shifted over the years at three miles/5000 metres. Using times of 14:00.0 for three miles and 14:30.0 for 5000 metres as his standard, Ross McWhirter revealed the following figures in terms of the accumulative number of athletes each country had produced at that level:

End of 1948: Sweden 17, Finland 15, Germany 5, USA 2.

End of 1952: Sweden 21, Finland 20, Germany 6, Great Britain 5, USA 5, Hungary 4, USSR 4, Yugoslavia 3.

End of 1954: Sweden 24, Finland 22, Great Britain 17, USSR 10, Hungary 9, Germany 8, Poland 5, USA 5, Belgium 4, Yugoslavia 4, Australia 3, Czechoslovakia 3, New Zealand 3.

Two Kenyans, Nyandika Maiyoro and Lazaro Chepkwony, had made a vivid impression at the AAA Championships and the Empire Games in Canada, beating that 14-min standard at three miles, but they were really only regarded as a quaint exotic sideshow. Ross McWhirter perceptively pointed out that of the 21 countries which had produced World-class men at three miles and 5000 metres it was Kenya which was the only newcomer in the two preceding seasons, but the athletics cognoscenti generally believed that the Hungarians - and most of all the worryingly frail-looking Iharos, who had set a European 1500 metres record and run the second fastest 3000 metres ever - were the men of the future.

For a year or so at least, the cognoscenti would be proved right.

12.

MORE WORLD-RECORD TARGETS IN 1955

The perfect picture of the rise and fall of the gladiators

EARLY IN 1955 J. Armour Milne again wrote at length about Zátopek in "Athletics Weekly", and it was fascinating stuff. Figures which he gave, presumably provided by Zátopek himself, revealed the extent of the runner's labours during the previous year and into the new year. Milne listed the following monthly training totals for 1954 in kilometres:

January 600, February 910, March 935, April 832, May 780, June 865, July 712, August 654, September 600, October 600, November 140, December 260. Total for the year 7,888.

Even for those long familiar with Zátopek's massive work load, this was breathtaking data. In March he had run 580 miles, averaging 145 miles a week. Even in June, having broken two World records, he ran 540 miles, averaging 135 a week. Having had his end-of-year wind-down, with a week off at Christmas-time, Zátopek had then proceded to run 1,057 kilometres in January 1955! That works out at an average of 165 miles a week! And all done in the depths of the Central European winter! Oh, by the way, Milne also broke the news that Zátopek now had a regular training companion, Ivan Ullsperger, who clearly enjoyed the partnership. Far from being overawed, he had outlasted Zátopek on occasions and had run 1,100 kilometres during that month!

Milne then went on to give a breakdown of Zátopek's schedule for the first three weeks of February:

Tuesday 1st: 40 x 400 metres (200 metres jogs)
Wednesday 2nd: 30 x 400 metres
Thursday 3rd: 2½ hours jogging & exercising indoors (bad weather)
Friday 4th: 30 x 400 metres, 1 hour jogging & exercising indoors (bad weather)
Saturday 5th: 10 x 400 metres, 1 hour jogging & exercising indoors (bad weather)
Sunday 6th: 2 hours jogging & exercising indoors (bad weather)
Monday 7th: 40 x 400 metres twice (!)
Tuesday 8th: 50 x 400 metres, 40 x 400 metres (!)
Wednesday 9th: 50 x 400 metres, 40 x 400 metres (!)
Thursday 10th: 40 x 400 metres twice (!)
Friday 11th: 40 x 400 metres twice (!)
Saturday 12th: 30 x 400 metres, 1 hour jogging & exercising
Sunday 13th: 2 hours jogging & exercising
Monday 14th: 5 x 200 metres, 20 x 400 metres, 5 x 200 metres "intensive" speed
Tuesday 15th: 5 x 200 metres, 20 x 400 metres, 5 x 200 metres "normal" speed
Wednesday 16th: 5 x 200 metres, 20 x 400 metres, 5 x 200 metres "intensive"
Thursday 17th: 5 x 200 metres, 10 x 400 metres, 5 x 200 metres "normal"
Friday 18th: 5 x 200 metres, 10 x 400 metres, 5 x 200 metres "intensive"
Saturday 19th: 5000 metres "easy", several short sprints
Sunday 20th: 8,300 metres road race, 1st 26:07.2, Tomis (2nd) and Šantrucek (3rd) both 26:19.2, Ullsperger (4th) 26:24.2.

So between Monday 7th and Friday 11th Zátopek had run 420 repetitions at 400 metres, which adds up to 168 kilometres! Taking further into account the 200 metres intervals in those sessions, and the training done on the other two days, Zátopek must have covered about 300 kilometres (180 miles) during the week! He was making no secret of the reason why he was training so hard in a non-Championship year. He had set himself the target of breaking his own records for six miles and 10,000 metres at Stará Boleslav on 14 May and then doing the same at 15 miles and 25,000 metres towards the end of the year.

At 32 his appetite for racing obviously remained unsated, but there was another strong political motivation for a man who had been promoted from Captain to Major after the 1952 Olympics, and then from Major to Lieutenant-Colonel in 1954, and who had also become an "Honoured Master of Sport". In 1955 it would be the 10th celebration of the Soviet Army's defeat of the Germans, and the anniversary of the liberation needed to be marked in the appropriate manner.

Milne, taking pains to remind readers of the fact that he had been resident in Eastern Europe since 1951 and that "I share their views", described Zátopek's day-to-day Army life as senior officer in charge of physical training and sport: "Zátopek is always to be found in his office or visiting an Army unit. He travels to work by tram. He walks to the stadium. He has no trainer dancing attendance upon him. He has no massage. After his training he takes a shower, walks to the tram, goes home. His home is a simple two-roomed flat with kitchen and bathroom. Apart from extremely generous financial support from the Government and much better organised Army sport (which is the core of the national sports movement so far as star athletes are concerned), athletics here has few advantages over athletics in Britain".

No doubt some of Zátopek's would-be emulators in Britain - such as bank-clerk-turned-salesman Pirie, for one - would retort to Milne that money and planning, such as was at Zátopek's disposal, was all that they needed to compete on more even terms.

Despite the vast amount of preparatory work put in, the 10,000-metre record attempt by Zátopek on 14 May failed. The weather conditions were totally unsuitable, and it seems odd that the organisers did not simply postpone the event until a better day, as they had done in the past. Milne reported that "it was cold beyond understanding for this time of the year". The wind was so strong that it was lifting dust clouds 20 or 30 yards into the air, and it rained three times during the race.

Ivan Ullsperger, acting as Zátopek's workhorse, ran splendidly to get to 5000 metres in 14:26.2 - only just outside the 14:25 target - but the pace slowed drastically once the record-holder was on his own, as the kilometre "splits" show: 2:51.0, 2:53.8, 2:53.0, 2:54.0, 2:54.4, 2:55.8, 2:58.4, 3:04.0, 3:05.0, 3:03.6. The finishing time of 29:33.0 was still highly commendable in the circumstances, but Milne's keen eye had spotted some deep-founded flaw. "Not all of the failure can be laid at the door of inclement weather," he wrote. "This was a Zátopek a long way short of his best. It is certain that he over-estimated his condition. It is possible, of course, that I had the unwelcome privilege of seeing the beginning of Zátopek on the way out, but I would not like to venture such an opinion".

The key reference in Milne's article was to the matter of Zátopek's over-estimation of his powers. This had always been his great forte ever since he had started out more than a decade before. He would set for himself only those targets which were attainable for him - even if they were beyond the reach of any other mortal being - and he would achieve them. If that ability had been lost with the passing of years, then Milne had indeed been the reluctant witness to a sad demise. Earlier that afternoon, in even worse weather, Josef Dolezal had proved that his new Zátopek-style training worked for him by adding over 100 metres to his record of three years previously for the two hours' walk. Little more than an hour after Zátopek had finished his run, the World record for 3000 metres was broken in Budapest by Sándor Iharos with a time of 7:55.6.

A fortnight later Ullsperger joined a select group when he beat his mentor quite easily over 5000 metres in Brno, 14:10.0 to 14:19.6, as the last occasion on which Zátopek had lost to a fellow-Czech at this distance had been in one of his very earliest races in 1944. At the Rošický Memorial Meeting in Prague on 9 June Ullsperger won again, 14:09.8 to 14:11.8, in a sprint over the last 200 metres and it seemed as if the 23-year-old acolyte was about to depose the high priest within his own diocese.

Being the sort of man he was, Zátopek's initial reaction would have been one of pleasure at his protegé's progress, but he was coldly realistic about his own form. Even after winning the 10,000 metres at the "International World Youth Games" in Warsaw in a wholly respectable time of 29:34.4, and in the process leaving Anufriyev (who had set a new national record of 29:10.6 in May) far behind, Zátopek was far from happy. One of the "international youth" present on the occasion, though strictly in a journalistic capacity, was Mel Watman, on his first overseas assignment, and he reported Zátopek in "Athletics Weekly" as saying dolefully, "I am no good this year". In the 5000 metres four days later he led for a short while but then finished a long way down. Jerzy Chromik, of Poland, won in 13:55.2 with Iharos and Kovács also under 14min. Zátopek was 6th, and one could only admire his courage for selflessly taking on what he must have known would be a hopeless task.

J. Armour Milne, also in the press tribune in Warsaw, wrote glumly of Zátopek: "In the 5000 metres he put in everything he had to try to come back to the speed which gave him a World record last year, but the inspiration just wasn't there, and he finished fighting hard but right out of the picture. Here, indeed, we saw the perfect picture of the rise and fall of the gladiators: Chromik wildly cheered by his own people; Zátopek walking from the arena quite unnoticed by the crowds".

There were nostalgic moments in the Czech match against France on 24-25 August for those who went to watch the old rivals described by Milne as the "two dwindling Olympians". Zátopek won the 5000 in 14:24.4 and Mimoun the 10,000 in 30:09.4, without either of them facing the other, and Milne commented, "For those who relish the battle of the gladiators, it was a disappointment. For others, with memories of greater days for both, it was a soothing pleasure to see both of the near-old-timers crossing the line first".

Yet against Poland, in Brno on 30-31 August, Zátopek overcame one of the fine young Polish runners, Krzyszkowiak, easily at 5000 metres and won the 10,000 the next day. In the 5000 Zátopek had been 15 metres down with 600 to go and then "got in one of his 'pulling the irons out of the fire' efforts, bagged the gallant Pole 350 yards out, and crushed him in one of his devastating last all-the-way sprints", according to Milne. "It wasn't the old Zátopek at his best, but nevertheless a good imitation of the 'old man' as he used to be". Then against Britain in Prague on 14-15 September he gave Pirie and Ken Norris a tremendous race at 5000, losing to Pirie, 14:03.8 to 14:04.0, and then beating him out of sight the next day at 10,000.

Zátopek's record bid at 15 miles and 25,000 metres was set for the official opening of the new "Stadium of Peace" at Celákovice on 29 October, and rather a lot was happening on the tracks of Europe in the weeks which preceded. In September Iharos had run a 5000 metres World record of 13:50.8, with a final kilometre of 2:41.2. Eight days later Kuts ran 13:46.8, with a final kilometre of 2:40.8. On 23 October Iharos, astoundingly, ran his last kilometre in 2:33.6 for a time of

13:40.6. The 5000 metres record, which had improved by 17.4 seconds in 15 years, had now been lowered by 16.6 seconds in less than 18 months.

The 1955 improvements had been made in the following manner, kilometre by kilometre:

Iharos, Budapest 10.09.55	2:44.0	2:49.4	2:49.8	2:46.4	2:41.2
Kuts, Belgrade 18.09.55	2:43.0	2:47.0	2:46.0	2:50.0	2:40.8
Iharos, Budapest 23.10.55	2:42.0	2:46.0	2:48.0	2:51.0	2:33.6

At 10,000 metres Zátopek's old rivals were closing in on his record. At the Czechoslovakia-Hungary match in Bratislava on 24 September Jozsef Kovács ran 29:02.6, with Zátopek three-quarters-of-a-minute down and according to Milne's mixed but apt metaphors "trying to fight his way through a sea of treacle, with the treacle steadily getting the upper hand". Kuts came even nearer with 28:59.2 in Bucharest on 3 October, and only a ninth kilometre in outside 3min cost him something quicker. "The writing is on the wall so far as this Zátopek record is concerned," said Milne.

Zátopek lost again at 10,000 metres to Gordon Pirie and Ken Norris in the London-v-Prague match on 12 October and at 5000 metres to Pirie in Manchester three days later, but with the record attempt on his mind - and defeat, it had to be said, no longer an exceedingly rare experience - the "dwindling Olympian" was still confident of a final flicker for the year.

Jimmy Green's report for "Athletics Weekly" of the London-v-Prague match (which Prague won by 110pts to 106) captured all the drama of a fog-bound evening at the White City. The meeting was to all intents and purposes a full-scale match between Great Britain and Czechoslovakia, and it was sponsored by the London "Evening News", whose benevolence extended to laying on a dinner afterwards for 250 guests at the Grosvenor House. Lord Burghley, the former Olympic 400 metres hurdles champion, proposed the toast of "The Match" and paid fulsome tribute to Zátopek in his speech, stating that "he had shown the World such fine qualities of sportsmanship".

ZÁ-TO-PEK! ZÁ-TO-PEK! ZÁ-TO-PEK!

Of the 10,000 metres race that night Green wrote as follows: "The eagerly-awaited 10,000 metres proved even more exciting than anyone could have expected. From the gun Zátopek went into the lead and his one objective was to run his opponents into the ground - tactics which paid dividends in Prague recently - but this time it was not to be. It was Zátopek, Pirie, Norris and Šantrucek until near the halfway mark, when the Czech second string was dropped. Just after the three-mile mark Pirie and Norris went by Zátopek, but they were soon re-passed, and though Pirie tried time and again to get by the Czech master held him off until the 17th lap, when Norris tore past and tried hard to get away but without shaking off either of the other two.

"Approaching 4½ miles Zátopek was up in front again, and by this time the other Czech runner, Šantrucek, was 100 yards behind. With four laps to go, Norris made another attempt and held the lead for two laps, then it was Zátopek again. He still led at the bell with the crowd tense with excitement. It was "Zá-to-pek! Zá-to-pek! Zá-to-pek!" - "Pi-rie! Pi-rie! Pi-rie!" - "Come on, Ken!" and anyone's race. I think, even at the bell, most people in the stadium thought the great Czech runner was going to win again, even though they hoped otherwise.

"But at 300 yards to go Pirie unleashed the finish he had been waiting for. He tore past and sprinted all the way for home, with Norris in hot pursuit but Zátopek a beaten man. He must have known at that moment that he could not respond to his younger rivals' challenge. To the accompaniment of some of the wildest cheering I have ever seen, Pirie tore home a comfortable winner in the good but not exceptional time - by World standards - of 29:19.0. Norris followed him home in as determined a fashion as I have seen, and he certainly lost no ground to Gordon in the last 150 yards.

"The time of the winner was the fastest ever in this country for 10,000 metres, though Pirie has accomplished a slightly better performance. It was interesting to note the remarkably even running of the race, despite the frequent bursts put in by the three leading runners. After the first mile, run in 4:44, the half-mile times were 2:23, 2:22, 2:22, 2:22.2, 2:20.8, 2:22, 2:23, 2:25, 2:22.

"It does look as though the great Czech master has reached the point where he is capable of being beaten by younger, speedier runners, though I would not suggest he is incapable of winning the 10,000 metres in Melbourne next year, but instead of being a certainty, or near certainty, the result is bound to be very open. In all probability, Vladimir Kuts is his most dangerous challenger - and Pirie's, too."

Almost half of the 20 pages of that issue of "Athletics Weekly" which carried the report on the London-Prague match was devoted to achievements by Czech athletes in one context or another, as extensive coverage was also given to Josef Dolezal beating the World record for the five miles' walk and Zátopek losing to Pirie at 5000 metres in the follow-up meeting at the former White City Stadium in Manchester three days later.

Even the editorial column was devoted to the same theme. "It is doubtful," pronounced Jimmy Green in heartfelt tones, "whether there has ever been a more popular athlete as a visitor to this country than Emil Zátopek. At a time when we are always being told that sportsmen from Communist countries have to win at any cost to enhance national prestige, it is nice to find such a charming personality who lives up to the highest traditions of British sportsmanship, both on and off the track. Win or lose, the famous Czech is always the same - a credit to his country and a credit to his sport.

"I know of no single individual who has done so much to improve the standard of his events - in this case one might say all the middle-distance and long-distance events. Now in the twilight of his career, he may not be gracing the tracks much longer and they will be the poorer for his departure. His name will live for ever in the annals of our sport".

Zátopek, no doubt philosophical about his losses and cheered by such a warm reception, had set himself a schedule for his record attempt later that month which called for 3:05 per kilometre and would give him a final time at 25,000 metres of 1:17:05. This was more than two minutes inside his own record from 1952 which had been the standard when he first laid his plans the previous winter, but somewhat surprisingly a runner from the USSR without any great credentials, Albert Ivanov, had achieved 1:17:34.0 in Moscow on 27 September. Maybe the Soviet Federation, knowing of Zátopek's intentions, thought they would lay claim to a record for at least a few weeks, but they erred in not taking a 15-mile time because Ivanov would certainly have had that record as well.

ZÁ-TO-PEK! ZÁ-TO-PEK! ZÁ-TO-PEK!

Zátopek ran with great skill - 10.2sec up on schedule at 5000 metres, 25.8sec up at 10,000 metres, 30.6sec up at 15,000 metres, 32.7sec up at 20,000 metres. His final times were 1:14:01.0 for 15 miles and 1:16:36.4 for 25,000 metres. Both records were to last a long time until Britain's Ron Hill finally broke them almost 10 years later. All in all, two World records and a No.1 World ranking represented another good season's work for the Zátopek household - but the No.1 ranking was for Dana, not Emil, with her 55.24m javelin throw which was only 24cm short of the World record. Emil had to settle for equal 11th at 5000 metres and eighth at 10,000 metres.

WORLD'S ALL-TIME BEST AT 5000 METRES

At the end of 1955:

13:40.6	Sándor Iharos (Hungary)	(1)	Budapest	23.10.55
13:46.8	Vladimir Kuts (USSR)	(1)	Belgrade	18.09.55
13:51.6	Chris Chataway (GB)	(1)	London	13.10.54
13:53.2	László Tábori (Hungary)	(2)	Budapest	23.10.55
13:55.2	Jerzy Chromik (Poland)	(1)	Warsaw	06.08.55
13:57.0	Emil Zátopek (Czecho)	(1)	Stockholm	03.09.54
13:57.6	Jozsef Kovács (Hungary)	(3)	Warsaw	06.08.55
13:58.2	Gunder Hägg (Sweden)	(1)	Gothenburg	20.09.42
13:58.8	Aleksandr Anufriyev (USSR)	(1)	Moscow	06.06.53
13:59.0	Miklós Szabó (Hungary)	(3)	Budapest	23.10.55

WORLD'S ALL-TIME BEST AT 10,000 METRES

At the end of 1955:

28:54.2	Emil Zátopek (Czecho)	(1)	Brussels	01.06.54
28:59.2	Vladimir Kuts (USSR)	(1)	Bucharest	03.10.55
29:02.6	Jozsef Kovács (Hungary)	(1)	Bratislava	24.09.55
29:10.6	Aleksandr Anufriyev (USSR)	(1)	Minsk	20.05.55
29:14.6	Ivan Chernyavskiy (USSR)	(1)	Kiev	02.10.55
29:17.2	Gordon Pirie (GB)	(1)	Stockholm	03.09.53
29:21.4	Ken Norris (GB)	(2)	London	12.10.55
29:23.0	Jerzy Chromik (Poland)	(1)	Lodz	25.10.55
29:23.8	Valter Nyström (Sweden)	(1)	Düsseldorf	14.09.52

| 29:24.8 | Herbert Schade (Germany) | (2) | Düsseldorf | 14.09.52 |
| 29:27.2 | Viljo Heino (Finland) | (1) | Kouvola | 01.09.49 |

Eagle-eyed statisticians will immediately notice that there are actually 11 names in the 10,000 metres list above, if only to accommodate the last of the Flying Finns for one more year. In the opening month of the Melbourne Olympic year of 1956, an Australian described as "The Flying Milkman" broke Zátopek's World record for six miles. Zátopek would have greeted the news with a cry of delight. The new record-holder was Dave Stephens, his dedicated disciple whom he had paced in Bucharest two years previously.

13.

THE OLYMPIC YEAR
OF 1956

Iron stamina, shuffling stride.
Sancho Panza's golden day at last

SERGEANT TOM McKIE, of the Glasgow city police force, was not the most obvious of sources for confirmation that Emil Zátopek was forsaking his long and honourable track career for a final fling at the marathon, but it was indeed Sgt McKie who was responsible for bringing that intelligence to the attention of the Western world.

Zátopek had made only fleeting appearances in Britain over the decade and the enterprising secretary of the Glasgow Police Sports, which for many years had been a meeting of major international importance attracting huge crowds, extended an invitation to him, along with Václav Janecek, Stanislav Jungwirth and Olga Modrachová to take part in the 1956 promotion in early June. A polite letter back from the Czech Federation gladly accepted the offer on behalf of the other three but added that the great man regretted he was unable to come.

In actual fact, Zátopek did run a handful of track races during the year and had even won a 5000 metres race in Bratislava on 5 June, finishing ahead of Milos Tomis by the narrowest of margins in 14:19.6, but later in the month he was beaten into 5th place at the Rošický Memorial meeting in Prague by Szabó, Kovács and two Czechs - an unexpected 28-year-old newcomer, Mïrko Graf, and Tomis again. Zátopek's one and only 10,000 metres of the year would not take place until 7 October, when he ran a solid if unspectacular 29:33.4.

These rare track outings may have seemed, at first impression, like token gestures. Zátopek, though, found it impossible to take any competition less than seriously and even in the Prague race he was "more often than not out in front and fighting every inch of the way", according to J. Armour Milne. At 4000 metres Szabó still had the past master on his shoulder and there must have been something of a shiver down the Hungarian's spine. Dana, carrying her age with the utmost grace, threw 52.24m on the second day of the Rošický meeting to stake her claim to defend her Olympic title.

Having started the year in the restored role of World record-holder at every distance from six miles to 30,000 metres, Zátopek had made a couple of cross-country appearances, finishing 3rd to Kuts and Chromik in the annual race organised in Paris by "*L'Humanité*", and then placing 2nd to Miroslav Koubek in the national championships - held on familiar territory in Gottwaldov. The International title had been won for the fourth time since 1949 by Alain Mimoun, and we would now, sadly, never know what Zátopek might have done in that sort of company.

The summer's activity on the track throughout Europe, with the Melbourne Olympics at the year's end as the major incentive, was immensely exciting. In sequence World records were set in the distance events as follows:

19 June, Bergen, 5000 metres: Gordon Pirie 13:36.8, beating Vladimir Kuts (13:39.6)

22 June, Trondheim, 3000 metres: Pirie 7:55.6 (equalling the record), beating Jerzy Chromik (7:56.4)

15 July, Budapest, six miles/10,000 metres: Sándor Iharos 27:43.8/28:42.8

4 September, Malmö, 3000 metres: Pirie 7:52.8, beating Iharos (8:05.8)

11 September, Moscow, 10,000 metres: Kuts 28:30.4

Kuts had led most of the way against Pirie in Bergen, and the kilometre "splits" there were 2:36.0, 2:46.0, 2:47.0, 2:48.0, 2:39.8. Iharos, running the 10,000 metres on the first day of the Hungarian championships, led Kovács by 60 metres after the first lap (!), and was already nine seconds up on record schedule at 3000 metres and 13.6 seconds up at halfway in an unprecedented 14:14.0. It was not, strictly speaking, his debut because he had run 33:04.4 in 1952, but it was the most radical achievement in the event since Zátopek's 29:02.6 in 1950.

Kuts had set a national record of 28:57.8 in early August and a subsequent record attempt was organised specially for him at a political rally attended by 100,000 people in Lenin Stadium. His early pace, as always, was phenomenal and at halfway he was on schedule for 28:16! This is how the most recent record-breaking runs of Zátopek, Iharos and Kuts compared, kilometre by kilometre:

Zátopek 28:54.2 in 1954
2:47.8   2:56.4   2:54.0   2:55.8   2:53.6   2:55.4   2:53.4   2:55.2   2:55.8
2:46.8

Iharos 28:42.8 in 1956
2:47.8   2:49.4   2:52.4   2:50.6   2:54.2   2:49.8   2:53.0   2:53.0   2:57.0
2:55.8

Kuts 28:30.4 in 1956
2:42.5   2:51.5   2:51.0   2:51.0   2:52.0   2:54.0   2:52.5.   2:54.0   2:54.0
2:47.9

The obvious advantage which Iharos had over Zátopek was that of basic speed. He had run 800 metres in 1:51.1 and 1500 metres in 3:40.8 (for a World record in 1955). Zátopek's best was 1:59.0 and 3:52.8. Iharos's coach, Mihály Igloí, had himself been a fine 1500 metres runner in the 1930s and had been a firm advocate of interval training ever since seeing the Polish Olympic 10,000 metres champion, Janusz Kusocinski, run 15 x 200 metres in a session during a visit to Budapest in 1933. So once Iharos's talents had been developed as a result of intensive interval work over a period of several years - and such training not needing to be as voluminous as Zátopek's because the natural speed was already in his legs - then the Hungarian was inevitably going to find it relatively easy to run successive kilometres in the best part of half-a-minute slower than the fastest of which he was capable.

However, the convenient theory that Zátopek's records were being beaten by men who were better 1500-metre runners does not apply so far as Kuts is concerned. He never ran faster than 3:52.0 - much the same as Zátopek - and the answer in his case is presumably that a dedicated system like that of the USSR with such a large and diverse population from which to choose was very likely to find sooner or later someone strong enough who could train as hard, or harder. The method worked twice, because Kuts's successor as Olympic champion and World record-holder at 10,000 metres was Pyotr Bolotnikov, also from the USSR.

The experts were in nevertheless no doubt that Zátopek would be the man to beat in the Olympic marathon, and that he was not going to Melbourne simply to enjoy a nostalgic reunion. The McWhirters stated categorically so in their preview in "Athletics World" but warned that there could be a familiar challenger: "If Colonel Zátopek is in shape there can be little doubt that, sentimentality apart, he must be the favourite for his fifth Olympic gold. He can still beat 29min 30sec for 10,000 metres. The greatest of all threats, however, if only he runs, must be Mimoun of France - his iron stamina, heat resistance and shuffling economic style mark him out to get his final revenge on Zátopek".

The qualifying remarks concerning Mimoun were not based on any doubts as to his fitness. On the contrary, at the age of 35 he had astonishingly improved his 10,000 metres best to 29:13.4 and it seemed as if he might even have the audacity to take on Kuts and Iharos at that distance. The other experts canvassed by the McWhirters were not convinced of Sancho Panza's ability to unseat at last Don Quixote. Dr Roberto Quercetani chose the Argentinian, Osvaldo Suárez, to win the marathon from Zátopek and the Finn, Karvonen. Dr Don Potts made the single choice of Zátopek. A fellow-American sage, Cordner Nelson, of "Track & Field News", forecast that Zátopek would win from Suárez and Karvonen. The McWhirters themselves named Zátopek, Kuznyetsov (USSR) and Karvonen in that order.

Kuts won the 10,000 metres in Melbourne on 23 November in 28:45.6, and Kovács and Al Lawrence (Australia) were both inside

ZÁ-TO-PEK! ZÁ-TO-PEK! ZÁ-TO-PEK!

Zátopek's old World record in the other medal places. Pirie was 8th, Mimoun 12th, Bolotnikov 16th, Stephens 20th. Iharos, apparently injured, was a non-starter. Kuts then won the 5000 metres five days later in 13:39.6 from Pirie and Derek Ibbotson. In 7th place was Maiyoro, of Kenya. In the women's javelin on the same day Dana missed a medal in 4th position by less than half-a-metre and another member of the Czech women's team, Olga Fikotová, attracted rather more headlines by winning the discus gold and starting a romance with the US hammer-throw gold-medallist, Hal Connolly.

The marathon was held on 1 December. The fastest of the 46 starters was Paavo Kotila, who had won the Finnish title in 2:18:04.8 from Oksanen (2:18:51.0) and Karvonen (2:18:56.4). Ivan Filin was the Soviet champion in 2:20:05.2. The classic annual Polytechnic race from Windsor to Chiswick, at which the now retired Jim Peters had set his World best times, had been won by Ron Clark, of Herne Hill Harriers, in 2:20:15.8. Also running were former track adversaries of Zátopek's such as Nyberg and Nilsson (both of Sweden), Mihalic (Yugoslavia) and Fred Norris (Great Britain). As Zátopek had not run in his national championship, won by Pavel Kantorek in 2:29:36.8, the state of his readiness to defend his title was something of a mystery. History was not in his favour, because no previous Olympic marathon champion had ever retained his title.

The race itself, by Olympian standards, was relatively uneventful. Mimoun was already up at the front at 15 kilometres, and at 20 kilometres (1:08:03) he was in a group of six including Filin, Karvonen and Mihalic, with Zátopek 10th. After halfway Mimoun was on his own and passed 30 kilometres in 1:41:47, but Zátopek was now up to 5th place within two minutes of the leader and by no means out of contention for the gold. Mimoun led Mihalic and Karvonen by over a minute at 35 kilometres and the positions stayed the same to the finish. Mimoun's winning time was exactly 2hr 25min and he waited the 4min 34sec until Zátopek came across the finishing line in 6th place. Zátopek took off his sun-cap and sank to his knees at the trackside, as if in supplication, and then the two old friends quietly embraced.

120

THE OLYMPIC YEAR OF 1956

On the eve of the 2000 Olympics in Sydney, and at the age of 79, Mimoun was invited back to Australia, and when he was taken into the scene of his triumph at the Melbourne Cricket Ground he caused his hosts some consternation by exuberantly divesting himself of his trousers and joyously running round the track in his underwear! Then, respectably donning the same No.13 vest and shorts he had worn to victory so many years before, he ran part of the marathon course again with a gaggle of admiring Australian schoolchildren.

The leading positions in the Melbourne Olympic marathon were as follows:

1 Mimoun (France) 2:25:00, 2 Mihalic (Yugoslavia) 2:26:32, 3 Karvonen (Finland) 2:27:47, 4 Chang Hoon Lee (Korea) 2:28:45, 5 Kawashima (Japan) 2:29:19, 6 Zátopek (Czechoslovakia) 2:29:34, 7 Filin (USSR) 2:30:37, 8 Nyberg (Sweden) 2:31:12, 9 Nilsson (Sweden) 2:33:33, 10 Oksanen (Finland) 2:36:10, 11 Vaide (Sweden) 2:36:21, 12 Choong Sik Choi (Korea) 2:36:53, 13 Kotila (Finland) 2:38:59, 14 Davies (South Africa) 2:39:48, 15 Hicks (GB) 2:39:55, 16 Hamamura (Japan) 2:40:53, 17 Richards (NZ) 2:41:34, 18 Russell (Australia) 2:41:44, 19 Beckert (Germany) 2:42:10, 20 Costes (USA) 2:42:20.

Altogether, only 33 of the 46 starters finished the course, and Zátopek was still too good for some of those who had so often trailed after him over the years. The Swedes, Nyberg and Nilsson, were 8th and 9th. A fellow Czech, Pavel Kantorek, was 27th. A pioneering Ethiopian, Bashay Feleke, was 29th. A Kenyan, Arap Sum Kanuti, was 31st. Among the non-finishers were Britain's Ron Clark and Fred Norris, Australia's Les Perry and the USSR's Albert Ivanov. The Argentinian, Suárez, so highly thought of by the pundits, did not appear at all at the Olympic Games that year but was 9th in the marathon in 1960.

Zátopek continued to race with unabated enthusiasm the following year, as if reluctant to let all the memories go and waste away too soon all that accumulated training resilience. He even ran 14:06.4 for 5000 and 29:25.8 for 10,000 metres. He ranked 24th for the year at 5000 metres. Two more Czechs, Jurek and Graf, were ahead of him and Kuts

ZÁ-TO-PEK! ZÁ-TO-PEK! ZÁ-TO-PEK!

led with another World record of 13:35.0. At 10,000 metres it was a quiet year: a Briton, George Knight, was fastest at 29:06.4; Kuts was ranked 3rd at 29:10.0; Zátopek was 11th, Kovács 25th, Mimoun 28th, Pirie 29th, Anufriyev 33rd and a Finn named Viljo Heinääho was 65th.

It was a lull before the storm.

At the 1960 Olympic Games in Rome the first eight men ran faster for 10,000 metres than Zátopek had ever done. Little more than a month later Pyotr Bolotnikov, the USSR's Olympic champion, set a World record of 28:18.8. At the year's end Zátopek was the 13th fastest man of all time - but not one among the dozen from eight different countries ahead of him would for one moment have denied his eternal debt of gratitude to the greatest distance-runner of his era. They had followed where he had led the way.

WORLD ALL-TIME BEST AT 10,000 METRES

At the end of 1957:

28:30.4	Vladimir Kuts (USSR)	(1)	Moscow (WR)	11.09.56
28:42.8	Sándor Iharos (Hungary)	(1)	Budapest (WR)	15.07.56
28:52.4	Jozsef Kovács (Hungary)	(2)	Melbourne (OG)	23.11.56
28:53.6	Al Lawrence (Australia)	(3)	Melbourne (OG)	23.11.56
28:54.2	Emil Zátopek (Czecho)	(1)	Brussels (WR)	01.06.54
29:05.0	Zdzislaw Krzyszkowiak (Pol)	(4)	Melbourne (OG)	23.11.56
29:06.4	George Knight (GB)	(1)	Warsaw	07.09.57
29:09.8	Pyotr Bolotnikov (USSR)	(1)	Moscow	29.08.57
29:10.0	Jerzy Chromik (Poland)	(1)	Warsaw	09.09.56
29:10.6	Aleksandr Anufriyev (USSR)	(1)	Minsk	20.05.55

WORLD ALL-TIME BEST AT 10,000 METRES

At the end of 1960:

28:18.8	Pyotr Bolotnikov (USSR)	(1)	Kiev (WR)	15.10.60
28:30.4	Vladimir Kuts (USSR)	(1)	Moscow (WR)	11.09.56
28:37.0	Hans Grodotzki (Germany)	(2)	Rome (OG)	08.09.60
28:38.2	Dave Power (Australia)	(3)	Rome (OG)	08.09.60
28:39.6	Aleksey Desyatchikov (USSR)	(4)	Rome (OG)	08.09.60

28:42.8	Sándor Iharos (Hungary)	(1)	Budapest (WR)	15.07.56
28:48.0	Murray Halberg (NZ)	(1)	Auckland	28.03.60
28:50.2	Max Truex (USA)	(6)	Rome (OG)	08.09.60
28:52.4	József Kovács (Hungary)	(2)	Melbourne (OG)	23.11.56
28:52.4	Zdzislaw Krzyszkowiak (Pol)	(7)	Rome (OG)	08.09.60
28:52.6	John Merriman (GB)	(8)	Rome (OG)	08.09.60
28:53.6	Al Lawrence (Australia)	(3)	Melbourne (OG)	23.11.56
28:54.2	Emil Zátopek (Czech)	(1)	Brussels (WR)	01.06.54
28:58.0	Aleksandr Artinyuk (USSR)	(1)	Moscow	03.07.60
28:58.6	Yevgeniy Zhukov (USSR)	(2)	Stockholm (ECh)	19.08.58

In 1964 African runners made their first appearance in the top 10 of all-time - Mohammed Gammoudi, of Tunisia, and Mamo Wolde, of Ethiopia. At the 2000 Olympics the first six finishers in the 10,000 metres were all African and by the end of the year 18 of the 20 fastest of all-time were African-born. Had Emil Zátopek and Haile Gebrselassie defied Father Time and somehow raced against each other at their best, Gebrselassie would have won by more than two laps. That is the brutal evidence of the statistics which allows such direct comparison between different generations. That does not necessarily mean, however, that Gebrselassie is the better runner.

WORLD ALL-TIME BEST AT 10,000 METRES

At the end of 2003:

26:22.75	Haile Gebrselassie (Ethiopia)	(1)	Hengelo (WR)	01.06.98
26:27.85	Paul Tergat (Kenya)	(1)	Brussels (WR)	22.08.97
26:30.03	Nicholas Kemboi (Kenya)	(2)	Brussels	05.09.03
26:36.26	Paul Koech (Kenya)	(2)	Brussels	22.08.97
26:38.08	Salah Hissou (Morocco)	(1)	Brussels (WR)	23.08.96
26:38.76	Abdullah Hassan (Qatar)	(3)	Brussels	05.09.03
26:49.38	Sammy Kipketer (Kenya)	(1)	Brussels	30.08.02
26:49.57	Kenenisa Bekele (Ethiopia)	(1)	St-Denis (WCh)	24.08.03
26:49.90	Assefa Mezegebu (Ethiopia)	(2)	Brussels	30.08.02
26:50.20	Richard Limo (Kenya)	(3)	Brussels	30.08.02
26:51.49	Charles Kamathi (Kenya)	(1)	Brussels	03.09.99
26:52.23	William Sigei (Kenya)	(1)	Oslo (WR)	22.07.94
26:52.30	Mohammed Mourhit (Bel)	(2)	Brussels	03.09.99
26:52.87	John Cheruiyot Korir (Kenya)	(5)	Brussels	30.08.02

ZÁ-TO-PEK! ZÁ-TO-PEK! ZÁ-TO-PEK!

26:58.38	Yobes Ondieki (Kenya)	(1)	Oslo (WR)	10.07.93
26:58.76	Sileshi Sihine (Ethiopia)	(3)	Hengelo	01.06.03
27:04.20	Abraham Chebii (Kenya)	(1)	Palo Alto	04.05.01
27:04.54	Felix Limo (Kenya)	(2)	Brussels	25.08.00
27:05.88	Patrick Ivuti (Kenya)	(6)	Brussels	30.08.02
27:06.17	John Yuda (Tanzania)	(7)	Brussels	30.08.02

All of these 20 fastest 10,000 metres runners ever are African. Abdullah Hassan was formerly Albert Chepkurui, of Kenya. Mohammed Mourhit was born in Morocco. The fastest non-African is Arturo Barrios (Mexico), with 27:08.23 in 1989, ranking 26th. The fastest European-born runner is Antonio Pinto (Portugal), with 27:12.47 in 1999, ranking 32nd. The fastest Czech or Slovak is Robert Štefko, of the Slovakian Republic, with 27:42.98 in 1997.

14.

A POIGNANT POSTSCRIPT

The race of progress: Zátopek 1, Clarke 2, Gebrselassie 3!

VLADIMIR KUTS WAS never the same man again after his stupendous efforts in 1956 and his World-record 5000 metres in 1957. He won no further medals, broke no more records, and died in 1975 at the age of 48. Gordon Pirie's career lasted another tempestuous five years, but his only medal was a European bronze at 5000 metres in 1958, and in those days of steadfast lip-service to the outdated ideals of amateurism he eventually finished up in the tawdry professional ranks as a sort of running toreador in Spanish bull-rings. He died in 1991 aged 60. Sándor Iharos, his life irrevocably torn apart by the 1956 Hungarian uprising, ran in the Olympics again in 1960, 10th at 5000 metres and 11th at 10,000 metres, and died in 1996 at the age of 65. The last of the Flying Finns, Viljo Heino, outstayed them all, living to the age of 84.

Emil Zátopek took part in a couple of low-key track races in 1958, including even a 10,000 metres event in Beijing (31:13.0 on 13 October), but ran his last significant international race in Spain in January of that year - and he finished with a grand flourish. George Knight, the World's fastest 10,000 metres man of the previous year, was the favourite for the annual San Sebastian cross-country event, but in warm and windy conditions it was Zátopek who got away on the last lap to win by fully 70 metres from the North African-born Frenchman, Hamoud Ameur. The leading Englishman, in 4th place 48 seconds behind Zátopek, was Alan Perkins, and at the International Cross-Country Championships in Cardiff two months later Perkins was again 4th - and only nine seconds down on the winner.

ZÁ-TO-PEK! ZÁ-TO-PEK! ZÁ-TO-PEK!

Pyotr Bolotnikov beat Kuts's 10,000 metres record in 1960 and again in 1962. Kuts's 13:35.0 for 5000 metres lasted rather longer until 1965. The records at both distances were surpassed by Ron Clarke, who had carried the torch into the Olympic Stadium in Melbourne. His and subsequent improvements of the records at 5000 and 10,000 metres have, of course, relegated all the historic performances of the 1950s to mere footnotes in the ranking-lists, but one interesting interpretation which can be made of the progressive improvements at 10,000 metres over the years is that Zátopek took the record on by 41.2 seconds from what it was before him, Clarke by 38.8 seconds, and Gebrselassie by only 29.48 seconds!

WORLD RECORD PROGRESSION DECADE BY DECADE AT 5,000 METRES AND 10,000 METRES

At the end of 1969:

> 13:16.6 - Ron Clarke (Australia) 1966
> 27:39.4 - Clarke 1965

At the end of 1979:

> 13:08.4 - Henry Rono (Kenya) 1978
> 27:22.4 - Rono 1978

At the end of 1989:

> 12:58.39 - Said Aouita (Morocco) 1987
> 27:08.23 - Arturo Barrios (Mexico) 1989

At the end of 1999:

> 12:39.36 - Haile Gebrselassie (Ethiopia) 1998
> 26:22.75 - Gebrselassie 1998

A POIGNANT POSTSCRIPT

On a single evening at the end of May 2004 - and at the same Hengelo track in Holland where he had set his 10,000 metres record six years before - Gebrselassie lost one record and was personal witness to another being closely threatened. The perpetrators were two of hs youthfully precocious fellow-countrymen. Kenenisa Bekele ran 12:37.35 for 50000 metres and Gebrselassie himself was beaten at 10,000 metres by Sileshe Sihine in a time of 26:39.69. Bekele and Sihine were both aged 21, and it must now be regarded as perfectly feasible that 12 minutes 30 seconds for 5000 metres and 26 minutes 15 seconds for 10,000 metres will be achieved within the very near future.

Zátopek's World records at the longer distances fared well. His 10 miles time survived from 1951 to 1961, his 20,000 metres and his hour from 1951 to 1963, his 15 miles and 25,000 metres from 1955 to 1965. His 30,000 metres record was beaten by Antti Viskari, of Finland, in 1956. In 1958 Miroslav Jurek improved on Zátopek's Czech record for 5000 metres with a time of 13:52.2. His 10,000 metres record was eventually removed by Josef Jánsky, with 28:43.2 in 1971. There was a sad symbolism to the latter occasion because by then Zátopek had been deprived of all his titles and honours by the repressive Czech regime after the failure of the 1968 rebellion.

In April of 1968 the newly appointed First Secretary of the Czech Communist Party, Alexander Dubcek, had introduced liberalising reforms under the title of "socialism with a human face". Among the signatories of Dubcek's "Manifesto of 2000 Words" were Emil and Dana Zátopek. Then the "Prague Spring" was brought to a brutal end on 20 August 1968, when 200,000 Soviet and Warsaw Pact troops entered the country.

Zátopek was stripped of his army rank and his Communist Party membership and spent many years working as a labourer with a geological survey team in a remote rural area of the countryside.

Yet even in those straitened circumstances his natural good humour seemed to carry him through. Though the authorities tried to deny foreign visitors access to him, Dr Roberto Quercetani met him at the 1978 European Championships in Prague and found him only too ready to discuss his athletics career, as referred to in the foreword to this book.

Stan Greenberg, a founder-member of the National Union of Track Statisticians and for many years the statistician for BBC Television, also came into contact with Zátopek on that occasion and remembers it fondly. "One evening Zátopek called in at the media hotel in Prague and was soon swamped by journalists eager to interview the great man. After talking to the British press for some time, he ended with an apology for 'my poor English'. He then went over to the Gallic press and conversed in good French before moving over to the Germans and talking easily to them. He was also conversant in Russian. To add to all this, he was a most pleasant and unassuming man and never seemed to lose his temper or raise his voice. When compared to most of the current crop of 'stars', he was a veritable giant.

"I was privileged to see him racing on a number of occasions and not least in Helsinki in 1952 when he achieved his unique and phenomenal triple. On a later occasion at the White City Stadium, in London, those of us who were Zátopek supporters cheered for the Czech runner despite our usual allegiance to Gordon Pirie, and our metronomic chant of 'Zá-to-pek! Zá-to-pek! Zá-to-pek!' left surrounding spectators wondering where all those Czechs had come from!

"Of all the many remarks which were attributed to Zátopek, there are a couple which I consider to be wonderful - 'For me a day without a visit to the track is like a meal without wine or a day without sun', and when asked why he grimaced when he raced he replied, 'I am not talented enough to run and smile at the same time'."

The fall of the Berlin Wall in 1989 led to a student uprising in Czechoslovakia, a general strike, and free elections in June 1990 when a former political prisoner, Václav Havel, became President. Zátopek was given a job reading foreign publications to help the Czech Sports Ministry keep pace with developments in training and techniques. Thus finished the working life of the man whose own training had inspired his entire generation and the one which followed.

He made a nostalgic and hugely-applauded appearance on the track as one of the guests at the 1992 Olympic Games in Barcelona. The slowest qualifier for the 5000 metres final there ran 20sec faster than he had ever done and the final itself was won in three-quarters of a minute faster than his best. The slowest qualifier at 10,000 metres ran almost 20sec faster than Zátopek's best ever, and in the final the first two men were over a minute faster than his ultimate World record.

A POIGNANT POSTSCRIPT

That same year, when he was interviewed shortly before his 70th birthday by the Slovak journalist, Ladislav Krnac, he reflected on his athletics career and his closest rivals and his inspirations. He recalled: "After the 5000 metres race at the 1946 European Championships one of our high-ranking officials pointed out to me that I had run faster than Paavo Nurmi ever did, and I still remember how elated I was at these remarks. Nurmi was my boyhood hero and I had always admired his dedication to athletics. In his days running had something of an artistic endeavour about it, whereas now everything seems to be ruled by science".

In the last year of his life he became increasingly frail and after suffering a heart attack was admitted to the army hospital in Prague where he died at the age of 78 on 21 November 2000. He and Dana had been married for 52 years.

15.

DANA WAS NOT SIMPLY "THE LITTLE WOMAN" EVER AT EMIL'S SIDE

17 years in World class. Finalist in four Olympics. Even Emil cannot match that!

THE EXQUISITELY NEAT juxtapositioning of gold-medal successes on the same day at the 1952 Helsinki Olympics has forever relegated Dana Zátopková to what might seem like the role of dutiful wife following in husband's footsteps. Yet, far from being in Emil's shadow, Dana deserves the fullest recognition as a Champion of Champions in her own right.

In some respects, she even surpasses the great man's achievements. Did she not, after all, compete in four successive Olympic Games - one more than Emil - and in doing so win a silver medal on her final appearance? Did she not, also, remain in the World rankings over a period of 17 years - three more than Emil - and continue to compete with distinction past her 42nd birthday?

In addition to winning the Olympic title in 1952, she was European champion in 1954 and 1958 and set a World record in the latter year. From 1949 to 1961 she was never lower than 7th in the annual World rankings, and throughout the 1950s she was the only consistent challenger in the event to the domination of a succession of Soviet women. Dana Zátopková remains, unquestionably, one of the greatest javelin throwers in the history of women's athletics.

DANA WAS NOT SIMPLY "THE LITTLE WOMAN"

As a teenager Dana (nee Ingrová) was a talented performer in athletics, swimming, gymnastics and volleyball - and she was particularly outstanding as a handball player. It was not until 1946, at the age of 23, that she took up javelin throwing, and the similarities with her future husband's early introduction to distance-running are uncanny. Handball was her preferred sport and she only became a javelin-thrower with some reluctance, in much the same way as Emil had to be cajoled into his first races. She was also to become a pioneering spirit in an event in which Czech women had not previously achieved anything of lasting note, just as Emil had no national tradition to follow in his events.

As a student at a physical education college Dana was sent on an athletics training course and was introduced to the javelin but found great difficulty in mastering the grip. It was only at the end of the session when the instructor saw her casually throwing 30 metres or so, holding the implement by instinct as if it was a fountain-pen, that her potential was realised. Before the end of the course she had thrown 34.70m and a fortnight later she won the national title with 35.64m!

The national record had been held by Anna Holíková at 36.52m since 1932, so Dana's startlingly sudden emergence was bound to cause a stir. Another Czech, Štefánia Pekarová, had competed prominently for several years in the 1930s and had actually thrown 43.49m in 1937, but later assumed a male role in life. During 1947 Dana, while also competing at 100 metres and in the high jump and discus, won the national javelin title again with 32.36 and threw a season's best of 36.05 in Cracow, in Poland.

In 1948, by which time her romance with Emil was blossoming, she was apparently required to throw 40.00m to qualify for the Olympic team, and she did that to the very centimetre to win the national title once more. At the Games she was a commendable 7th with 39.64 on the day after Emil had won the 10,000 metres and the same day that he ran his 5000 metres heat. Even allowing for the absence of the USSR from the Games, this was a fine performance; the title was won with a throw of 45.57m by 33-year-old Herma Bauma, of Austria, who had placed 4th at the 1936 Games.

David Thurlow, the athletics historian whose memories go back more than 50 years, has a particularly fond recollection of Zátopek. Emil set off on the London underground railway to Uxbridge to seek out Dana at the separate lodgings for the women competitors. Strictly no fraternisation was allowed, and as she looked down from a window he proudly waved his gold medal at her. Unfortunately, in his excitement he managed to drop the medal into the swimming-pool by which he was standing, but undeterred he stripped to his underpants and dived in and retrieved his prize. Because it was Zátopek, the officials made no fuss about such a flagrant breach of etiquette and propriety!

Dana's best throw for the year was 40.65 in Vienna on 12 September (when Herma Bauma set a ratified World record of 48.63) and soon afterwards her marriage to Emil took place and she moved to Prague. There she began training with an intensity that few women in the event, if any, outside the USSR could ever have matched. She regularly threw the men's javelin in training and managed to master the all-important art of transferring her impetus from the run-up to the throwing phase. Her improvement in 1949 was immense: to 42.00 in Cracow on 19 June, 44.02 in Brno on 16 July and 46.32 in Bucharest on 10 September. The USSR was now affiliated to the IAAF and Natalya Smirnitskaya had set an official World record of 53.41 in Moscow in August.

Early in 1950 the Zátopeks were invited to the training camp at the Black Sea resort of Sochi which was being staged for the leading Soviet athletes, and there, according to František Kozík, Dana learned a lot from the javelin coaches and from watching Smirnitskaya lifting and throwing heavy weights in training. Dana's best throw for the 1950 season was 48.43 in Bratislava on 9 July. She ranked 5th in the World, and all four ahead of her were from the Soviet Union; the great all-rounder, Aleksandra Chudina, led at 51.56 from Smirnitskaya (50.98), Galina Zybina (50.67) and Vera Nabokova (50.10). At the European Championships in Brussels Dana was not at her best, finishing 5th with 41.34 behind Smirnitskaya (47.55), Bauma, Zybina and Nabokova.

Dana's best for 1951 was a further personal best of 49.90, set in the match against Hungary in Budapest on 25 August at which Emil won both the 5000m and 10,000m. Only three others, all from the USSR, ranked ahead of her for the year, led at 51.45 by Zybina - a future Olympic champion and multi-World record-holder in the shot. On the all-time list, still headed by Smirnitskaya at 53.41, Dana was 7th behind six Soviet throwers.

DANA WAS NOT SIMPLY "THE LITTLE WOMAN"

During the winter of 1951-52 she trained more strenuously than ever before. She threw outdoors in all weathers - often 40 or 50 throws of a 1kg iron bar out to around the 40-metre mark, as if she was matching every one of Emil's 40 or 50 repetitions at 400 metres. She was also running for sprint speed (10 x 50 metres flat out, with 150-metre jogs) and for stamina, was high jumping, and was exercising in the gymnasium with the men's 16lb shot. Emil was not alone on his snowbound track session. Nor would he be alone, Dana must have been promising herself, on the Olympic rostrum.

Having seen Emil win his second gold medal in Helsinki at 5000 metres on 24 July, Dana began her javelin competition a few minutes later with Chudina, Zybina and Yelena Gorchakova as her Soviet opponents and the defending champion, Herma Bauma (now 37), also taking part. As if emulating one of Emil's crushing fast starts to a race, Dan threw her best ever of 50.47 in the first round to lead by almost four metres and the nearest approach for the rest of the evening came from Chudina, with 50.01 on her final effort. The full result was as follows:

1 Zátopková (Czechoslovakia) 50.47, 2 Chudina (USSR) 50.01, 3 Gorchakova (USSR) 49.76, 4 Zybina (USSR) 48.35, 5 Kelsby (Denmark) 46.23, 6 Müller (Germany) 44.37, 7 Ciach (Poland) 44.31, 8 Kruger (Germany) 44.30, 9 Bauma (Austria) 42.54, 10 Puente (Uruguay) 41.44, 11 Turci (Italy) 41.20, 12 Bausenwein (Germany) 41.16, 13 Larney (USA) 40.58, 14 Rattyä (Finland) 40.56, 15 Coates (GB) 40.17, 16 Parviainen (Finland) 39.82, 17 Torikka (Finland) 39.58.

The 1953 World rankings were led by Chudina (52.75) and Nadyezhda Konyayeva (52.26), with Zátopková 3rd at 52.02, set in Prague on 13 June (Emil won a 5000 metres at the same meeting). Then, in preparation during 1954 for the European Championships in Berne the 22-year-old Konyayeva threw successive World records of 53.56 in February, 55.11 in May and 55.48 in early August. Dana's best prior to the Championships was 53.26 in Prague on 28 July.

After the first round in Berne Konyayeva led with 49.08. Dana was 2nd at 47.65 but then proceeded to throw beyond 50 metres in all of the remaining five rounds, stretching her lead with 51.65, 52.07 and then

ZÁ-TO-PEK! ZÁ-TO-PEK! ZÁ-TO-PEK!

52.91. As the javelin competition reached its latter stages, Dana was no doubt casting an occasional glance at what was happening on the track because Emil was running away with the 10,000 metres title. The result of the women's javelin was as follows:

1 Zátopková (Czechoslovakia) 52.91, 2 Roolaid (USSR) 49.94, 3 Konyayeva (USSR) 49.49, 4 Kruger (Germany) 47.39, 5 Chudina (USSR) 47.05, 6 Kalusevic (Yugoslavia) 46.78, 7 Majka (Poland) 44.80, 8 Vigh (Hungary) 43.74, 9 Brömmel (Germany) 42.39, 10 Almqvist (Sweden) 41.95, 11 Gross (Germany) 41.47, 12 Reimesch (Rumania) 41.36, 13 Kelsby (Denmark) 40.78, 14 Schwartzler (Austria) 35.28.

In 1955 Dana led the World rankings for the first time with a throw of 55.24 which was very close to Konyayeva's World record, and her successes during the year included an easy win in the London v Prague match at the White City, but in 1956 she was never quite in prime form. Her best for the year was 52.24 in June and at the Olympic Games in Melbourne in November she was 4th with 49.83. The first three were Inesa Jaunzeme (USSR) with 53.86, the very surprising Marlene Ahrens (Chile) with 50.38, and Konyayeva with 50.28.

The 1957 season was much better for Dana as she ranked 2nd in the World with 53.80 to Zybina's 54.81. Dana steadily improved from 53.00 in Bucharest on 23 June, to 53.42 in Gottwaldov on 22 September, 53.62 in Brno on 12 October and then her 53.80 in Prague on 19 October. Of the 10 longest throws in the World during the year she had four and Zybina only one.

For the European Championships year of 1958 Dana's form was her best yet at the age of 35 - and could that be because husband Emil was now virtually retired and she could concentrate all her attentions on her own career? She began with throws of 54.77, 54.17 and 54.16 in May, and then on 1 June at the Strahov Stadium, in Prague, where Emil had enjoyed so many of his finest runs, she at last broke the World record with a first-round throw of 55.73. The record-breaking effort came about at the unlikely time of 11.10 in the morning and she had three more throws in the 53-to-54m range. The record only lasted 54 days because the Polish-born Anna Pazera, of Australia, won the Empire Games title in Cardiff in July with a totally unheralded 57.40.

DANA WAS NOT SIMPLY "THE LITTLE WOMAN"

The nearest approach by Europeans to Dana's best at that stage of the season was 54.98 by Zybina, 54.66 by Jutta Neumann (Germany) and 54.10 by Almut Brömmel (also Germany). The 14 competitors at the European Championships in Stockholm (excluding Zybina, who was absent) between them had 48 throws, but the event was to all intents and purposes completed with still 41 throws to come. Birute Zalogaitite, of the USSR, had led with 50.71 in the first round, but then Dana launched the javelin out to a European record of 56.02, and no one else came remotely close. The result was as follows:

1 Zátopková (Czechoslovakia) 56.02, 2 Zalogaitite (USSR) 51.30, 3 Neumann (Germany) 50.50, 4 Bogun (USSR) 49.88, 5 Grabowska (Poland) 49.77, 6 Figwer (Poland) 49.48, 7 Diti (Rumania) 49.03, 8 Brömmel (Germany) 48.85, 9 Almqvist (Sweden) 46.90, 10 Kipp (Germany) 46.89, 11 Tsvetkova (USSR) 45.52, 12 Kalusevic (Yugoslavia) 45.42, 13 Starzynska (Poland) 45.10, 14 Williams (GB) 44.04.

In subsequent meetings Dana won with 53.17 in Oslo (25 August), 53.43 in Gothenburg (28 August), 55.88 against Hungary in Budapest (6 September), and another European record of 56.67 in Bucharest (13 September). Of the 20 leading throws of the year she had 10 whilst Zalogaitite had three and Zybina two, but she still ended up 3rd in the World rankings for the year because the 23-year-old Lithuanian-born Zalogaitite became the third different World record-holder that year with 57.49 in Tbilisi on 30 October.

Though now 36, Dana forged on for another six years after that, accumulating 13 national titles and winning the silver at the 1960 Olympics behind yet another Soviet World record-holder, Elvira Ozolina, who had thrown 57.92 and 59.55 in previous months. At those Rome Olympics Dana's Czech team-mate, Vlasta Pešková, placed 4th. The result of that final was as follows:

1 Ozolina (USSR) 55.98, 2 Zátopková (Czechoslovakia) 53.78, 3 Kalediene (USSR) 53.45, 4 Pešková (Czechoslovakia) 52.56, 5 Figwer (Poland) 52.33, 6 Pazera (Australia) 51.15, 7 Platt (GB) 51.01, 8

ZÁ-TO-PEK! ZÁ-TO-PEK! ZÁ-TO-PEK!

Shastitko (USSR) 50.92, 9 Antal (Hungary) 50.25, 10 Diti (Rumania) 49.56, 11 Gerhards (Germany) 49.27, 12 Ahrens (Chile) 47.53, 13 Oldham (USA) 46.52.

There was also a particularly good year for Dana in 1961, with 3rd ranking in the World at 56.10, and her "juniors" such as Kalediene (nee Zalogaitite), Gorchakova, Jaunzeme, Pöldsam (nee Roolaid) and Brömmel were all well behind her. In her final years, 1963 and 1964, Dana was still over 50 metres, and she set World best performances in every age group from 35 to 42. By then Ozolina had taken the World record to 61.38 and Gorchakova had improved that to 62.40 in the qualifying round at the Tokyo Olympics.

Dana Zátopková's javelin career

Olympic Games
1948 7th 39.64. 1952 1st 50.47. 1956 4th 49.83. 1960 2nd 53.78.

European Championships
1950 5th 41.34. 1954 1st 52.91. 1958 1st 56.02.

Year-by-Year World Ranking

1946 35.64 (-)
1947 36.05 (-)
1948 40.65 (30)
1949 46.32 (5)
1950 48.43 (5)
1951 49.90 (4)
1952 50.47 (3)
1953 52.02 (3)
1954 53.26 (3)
1955 55.24 (1)
1956 52.24 (5)
1957 53.80 (2)
1958 56.67 (3)

DANA WAS NOT SIMPLY "THE LITTLE WOMAN"

1959 54.09 (7)
1960 55.74 (3)
1961 56.10 (3)
1962 47.47 (-)
1963 50.96 (33)
1964 51.12 (46)

World All-Time Best Performers: Women's Javelin

At the end of 1960

59.55	Elvira Ozolina (USSR)	(1)	Bucharest (WR)	04.06.60
57.77	Urszula Figwer (Poland)	(1)	Koblenz	21.08.60
57.49	Birute Zalogaitite (USSR)	(1)	Tbilisi (WR)	30.10.58
57.40	Anna Pazera (Australia)	(1)	Cardiff (BEG/WR)	24.07.58
56.67	Dana Zátopková (Czecho)	(1)	Bucharest	13.09.58
56.21	Vlasta Pešková (Czecho)	(1)	Prague	19.06.60
55.73	Inesa Jaunzeme (USSR)	(1)	Tallinn	18.06.60
55.64	Inge Schwalbe (Germany)	(1)	Halle	10.07.60
55.59	Yelena Gorchakova (USSR)	(2)	Krasnodar	29.09.60
55.48	Nadyezhda Konyayeva (USSR)	(1)	Kiev (WR)	06.08.54

16.

ZÁTOPEK TALKS ABOUT STYLE, TRAINING, AMBITION, RECORD-BREAKING AND MASS SPORT

ZÁTOPEK TALKS ABOUT STYLE:
"When I began they said the way I ran was impossible"

"In my opinion style is only the outward aspect of a performance. It seems to me that it's superficial to judge an athlete by his style. Imagine that two athletes are racing at 5,000 metres - one of them in good style, and the other in poor style. Suddenly, one of them really lets fly and wins by 50 metres. What would you give as the reasons for his victory? His outward style or his inner qualities? And what if it just happens to be the one with the poor style who wins? How often has it happened that an athlete with a so-called classical style has never achieved anything very much? I have so often been criticised for not having a beautiful style. My answer has always been that I shall learn to have a better style once they start judging races according to their stylishness. So long as it's a question of speed, then my attention will be directed to seeing how fast I can cover the ground. When I began, they used to say that the way I ran was impossible. Then when I started to break records the critics said that was the way to do it!"

ZÁTOPEK TALKS ABOUT TRAINING:
"It's the speed of endurance that's vital"

"They used to say that several kilometres in succession was a feat of endurance. I'm not interested in how long I can hold out, but in how fast I can reach the finishing-line. So what I mean by endurance is the length of time I can maintain racing speed. For instance, if I can run 100 metres a number of times in 15 seconds that means that I can run 800 metres in two minutes. It also means I can do 1500 metres in 3min 45sec. It's the speed of endurance that is decisive in the event. I usually begin the season by seeing how much I can endure. For instance, 10 x 100 metres, 10 x 200 metres or 6 x 400 metres. Then as time goes on and I feel my powers of endurance growing, I stiffen the training. If it's raining? It doesn't matter. If I'm tired? That's irrelevant. If I can stick to the training throughout many long years willpower is no longer a problem".

ZÁTOPEK TALKS ABOUT AMBITION:
"Always keep within the bounds of the possible"

"I certainly think that an important factor in my success has been that I never over-rated my powers. I set myself tasks that I was capable of fulfilling. At the start it never occurred to me that one day I might stand on the Olympic victor's rostrum. Yet now youngsters write to me and tell me how much they already want to be there. I'm afraid they will not get very far. Perhaps I found that the right way to solve the problem was that one can only increase the effort step by step, and you must always keep within the bounds of what is possible. When I began to run, my comrades used to be able to beat me whenever they wanted. I was certainly not particularly talented. So I had to set my aims in relation to the superiority of others, and in doing so I was not thinking of records, and still less of the Olympics. My aims were such that given a slight improvement in form I could manage to achieve them. That's how I carried on, step by step, for many years. A good performance is not achieved by a single tremendous effort of willpower but by continuous effort".

ZÁTOPEK TALKS ABOUT RECORD-BREAKING:

"The fight against a new abstract opponent"

"To begin with I tried to beat my friend, Krupiçka, who was the club champion, and I would never have dared to race against the record-holder, Šalé. By degrees things went better. My stamina increased. My performances improved from race to race, but it wasn't particularly gratifying to me that I'd done as well as my teachers. To do better was much harder. I'd been able to follow in somebody else's footsteps until then, but to do better I had to make my own way. I had to work out what my training should be in order to increase my level of performance, and it wasn't easy. It was only when I discovered my weaknesses that I was able to overcome the lethargy which always set in after any outstanding success. After I had broken a record for the first time, I had to find new methods all over again. I had to take up the fight against a new abstract opponent - against myself. I'm not particularly interested in beating my opponents. Above all, I'm interested in improving my own performances. So why should I profit from my opponents' weakness and run worse times if I'm capable of doing better?"

ZÁTOPEK TALKS ABOUT MASS SPORT:

"I still want to improve ... it is a duty to our people"

"I'm glad if athletics is influencing young people. Of the many youngsters who have decided to devote themselves to athletics very few will mature to become record-holders, but their efforts will not be the less worthwhile, and I'm convinced that such mass participation will in the end have a great influence on our people. Once, when I was received by President Gottwald, he said in his speech that the chief aim must be to devote ourselves to the broad masses, as well as giving care and attention to the leading sportsmen and sportswomen. All those who've achieved a leading position in their sport should try and attract newcomers to it. In spite of all the success I have had, I still want to improve my performances. I feel it is a duty to our people, and it is my thanks to them for the tremendous interest they take in my racing. Breaking records is not just my own affair. The common will is pressed upon me and I'm driven on to greater efforts by it".

The above extracts are edited versions of interviews with Emil Zátopek by František Kozík which appeared in his biography, "Zátopek The Marathon Victor", published by ARTIA, Prague, in 1954.

17.

AN APPRECIATION: BY COLIN YOUNG

Emil Zátopek, as I knew him, for 45 years

WHETHER IT WAS seeing him compete at Wembley, in Berne or at the White City, or meeting him in London at the Windsor Hotel or in Soho Square, at the training track at the Rome Olympics, or many years later in Prague, I was always uplifted mentally and physically by the presence of Emil. His influence on my attitude to training, racing and athletics generally was immense, and it has lasted right up to this day - over more than half-a-century.

I particularly remember four occasions when his encouragement and enthusiasm for my humble efforts carried me through years of daily training and hundreds of races and gave me the determination to do my utmost, whatever the circumstances.

Meeting him and his great friend, Josef Dolezal, who was the walking 'Zátopek' throughout the 1950s, in London on the occasion of the 1955 London-v-Prague match was the first time that I had the opportunity of encountering Emil face-to-face. Four years later I travelled to the World Youth Festival held at the Prater Stadium, in Vienna, specifically to meet Emil and the ever-smiling and resilient Dana, and during a long discussion I enjoyed his many reminiscences of races he had run and characters he had met during his career. At the 1960 Rome Olympics as the US race-walker, Ron Laird, and I trained within the village Emil took time to jog and talk with us during our session. Some 30 years later I was fortunate enough to discuss with him in Prague details of many of his major Championship races.

AN APPRECIATION: BY COLIN YOUNG

Regarding the 1948 Olympic 5000 metres final, Emil clearly recalled how he had focussed on the Dutchman, Willy Slijkhuis, because he was so impressed with his finish. Slijkhuis had comfortably beaten Emil at 3000 metres in 1946 and 1947, though Emil had set a national record on each occasion. At Wembley Emil was surprised by the fierceness and timing of the attack by the Belgian, Gaston Reiff, which caught him at a low point when he was content to hang on to Slijkhuis, as he was feeling the effects of his previous exertions and the inclement conditions.

When recalling the 1954 European Championships 5000 metres, Emil said that he had realised after racing Vladimir Kuts in Bucharest the previous year that he would not be able to hold the aggressive front-runner with him concentrating on the shorter distance - particularly after his own 10,000 metres victory and the manner in which Kuts had attacked in the 5000-metre heats. During the final, with Kuts running at World-record pace, Emil concentrated on trying to outwit Chris Chataway for 2nd place but lacked enough finishing power.

However, what always amazed Emil was that just four days later he had recovered sufficiently to run his best ever time at the distance (13:57.0), despite the post-Berne celebrations, the travelling to Sweden, and the lonely race which he won by 35sec.

It is well known that Emil always had great regard for his fellow competitors, but in our conversations he often singled out one man who he believed was under-rated - the diminutive Jozsef Kovács, of Hungary. Emil said that whenever he raced the Hungarian he always had difficulty in dropping him and was always quick to point out that it was this man who was the first to beat him at 10,000 metres. Emil remained convinced that but for the 1956 Hungarian uprising Kovács would have gone on to greater achievements.

When discussing his renowned training methods Emil was at pains to point out that over the years a large proportion of his running was done on forest trails, often undulating and with approximate distances, varying intervals and untimed. In later years he thought he would have benefited from faster, more regimented sessions at certain times of the year.

He always considered that his 20,000 metres, when he ran 59:51.8 in 1951 on one of his favourite tracks at Stará Boleslav, was his finest

ZÁ-TO-PEK! ZÁ-TO-PEK! ZÁ-TO-PEK!

World record and in later years he thought that a 2:15 track marathon may well have been within his compass if he had been in top condition in 1956-57. He said that he always enjoyed lapping the track at a comfortable (!) pace when setting his long-distance records. He recalled that his last competitive race abroad was a cross-country event in which the British international, Alan Perkins, also competed.

On a personal note, Emil was delighted to discover that I had married a Czech (a Moravian, in fact, like Emil) and was proud to tell me that he was undefeated in races at Trebíc, which was my wife's home town, having lapped the field on the three occasions he won the annual 10,000 metres event there in 1949-50-51.

Of all the great runners who have followed in his wake, Emil singled out Ron Clarke and Haile Gebrselassie as his particular favourites. His admiration of their versatility, dominance, joy of running and humility knew no bounds, and he spoke in awe of the times which they had achieved. Yet all serious students of athletics know only too well that the great man's Helsinki Olympic "triple" at 5000 metres, 10,000 metres and the marathon will never be duplicated - and nor will the sheer *joie de vivre* which Emil always expressed. He was truly unique.

Colin Young was a founder-member of the National Union of Track Statisticians in Great Britain in 1958 and was an international race-walker of renown who was the only British competitor ever to complete the Paris-Strasbourg event. He was also coach to a British athlete, Mel Batty, who was one of those to subsequently improve on Emil Zátopek's one-time World record for 10 miles. A lifelong enthusiast for all aspects of athletics, Colin remains one of the most fervent of Emil's legion of fans throughout the World.

18.

AN EVALUATION:
BY MEL WATMAN

The personification of all that is worthy
in sport ... and in life

TRACK AND FIELD fans love to compare the merits of past champions with those of the current era to determine who is the greatest athlete of all time. It's a futile, subjective but enjoyable exercise, but I will guarantee that every knowledgeable enthusiast who has more than a stopwatch for a heart will have the name of Emil Zátopek at or near the top of their list.

One could argue that Haile Gebrselassie has by now overtaken Zátopek and Paavo Nurmi as the most consistently successful long-distance track runner the World has ever seen, or that Carl Lewis's achievements outshine those of every other athlete, but there should be more to this than mere facts and figures. Zátopek was an exceptional athlete, agreed, but transcending that was his humanity.

He was the personification of all that is worthy in sport, and in life. He was ambitious and successful but never lost his humility or sense of wonder. He had the capacity to enjoy himself and enrich the lives of others but also a stoicism born of early hardship which carried him through the bad times when he found himself on the wrong side of the political fence. His courage, on and off the track, was remarkable.

As a runner Zátopek broke through the barriers of what was deemed humanly possible by dint of training much harder than anyone before him and by pushing himself closer to the limits than his rivals. He was an uncompromising opponent who could destroy the field from the front,

145

as in most of his 10,000m races, or by summoning a fearsome kick, as in the classic 1952 Olympic 5000m. He won every honour during a long career and yet remained an intensely modest man, always somewhat bemused that long after his retirement he would still be recognised and honoured wherever he travelled.

His tortured expression and torso-rolling action, each stride looking as though it would be his last before collapsing, endeared him to fans the world over. Even his closest rivals, like Alain Mimoun and Gordon Pirie, had enormous affection as well as respect for the man dubbed "The Human Locomotive" and "The Bouncing Czech". His open, friendly personality won over everybody. He was always happy to share his training "secrets" and even in Olympic heats he would encourage or joke with his fellow competitors in a bewildering variety of languages. Such was his aura that even hard-bitten journalists would queue patiently to secure his autograph. Many an outstanding athlete is admired, hero-worshipped even ... Emil Zátopek was universally loved.

It was almost 40 years ago, in the first edition of my book, "The Encyclopaedia of Athletics", that I wrote: "In the eyes of many athletics experts, Emil Zátopek's triple triumph at the 1952 Olympics represents the sport's supreme achievement. Even to attempt the 5000m, 10,000m and marathon against the cream of the World's athletes is startling. To win all three - each in Olympic record time - is well nigh incredible". Nothing has changed since then to revise that opinion.

Another of Zátopek's legendary feats which surely will never be matched is his win-streak at 10,000m. Haile Gebrselassie, a worthy successor both on the track and by virtue of his winning personality, did not lose a race at that distance for seven years, a stunning achievement. But his sequence covers 11 races, whereas Zátopek won a phenomenal 38 consecutive races at 10,000 metres between May 1948 and July 1954! He then lost one close race before winning another nine on the trot for 47 victories out of 48.

On a personal note, although I was too young to see Zátopek at his zenith in the Helsinki Olympics, I was privileged to watch my hero in a few races towards the end of his career. It was largely due to the enticing prospect of viewing him in action at the 1955 World Youth Festival in Warsaw that, at 17, I made my first trip abroad and had my first by-lined report published in "Athletics Weekly", an event which was to determine the direction of my journalistic career.

For perhaps the best example of Zátopek's character and generosity we turn to another legendary distance runner, Ron Clarke, a man who set a stack of world records but never managed to win a major title. Writing in "Athletics Weekly" in 1987, the Australian recalled the end of his first visit to Zátopek nearly 20 years earlier:

"As he marched me through customs and onto the plane on my way out of Prague, he shook hands and, in so doing, secretly transferred a small package into my grip. I thought I was smuggling some message to the outside World for him, so did not dare open the little parcel until the plane was well outside Czechoslovakian territory. When I opened it up, it was his 1952 Olympic 10,000 metres gold medal. I thought back to the words he said as he passed it across to me, which at the time I did not understand: 'Because you deserved it', he said. I wish I had.

"I do know no-one cherishes any gift more than I do, my only Olympic gold medal, and not because of what it is, but because of the man whose spirit it represents".

Mel Watman is one of the most knowledgable and respected of international athletics journalists and is the editor of the prestigious newsletter, "Athletics International". Like Colin Young, he is a founder member of the National Union of Track Statisticians, and he is also a member of the Worldwide Association of Track and Field Statisticians. Among the many authoritative publications to his name are "The Encyclopaedia of Athletics" and "Who's Who in World Athletics".

19.

A POSTSCRIPT:
BY NEIL ALLEN

My clandestine meeting with the fiery "little stoker"

ONE OF THE MANY full-length obituaries of Emil Zátopek which appeared in the British press after he died in November 2000 at the age of 78 claimed that the four-time Olympic gold-medallist from the then Communist state of Czechoslovakia was not allowed to talk very freely, if at all, to western journalists even in his early years of retirement from the track. Yet he quickly found a way out of that when I met him at a reception at the British Embassy in Prague during the mid-1960s.

After a few minutes of friendly chat, Zátopek suddenly lowered his voice. "Look, my friend, our secret police don't really like me staying too long in a place like this. But I've got my car outside, so why don't you come with me and I'll take you for a tour of my wonderful old city, and we'll talk as much as you like".

To this day I cannot quite believe that it happened as easily as that, but then Emil was always the most approachable of all the heroes of our sport, ready with a smile or even a hug for anyone who encountered him. I was to meet him several times more - once even in the Czechoslovak Embassy in London where Mick Jagger's father, who was a former physical education lecturer, was among the admiring throng.

Nothing, though, was ever so captivating as that joyful hour's drive round golden *Praha* as my driver bubbled with memories of Wembley in 1948 and displayed all his zest for life and international friendship. Here, with acknowledgment to "The Times", of which I was athletics correspondent for 20 years, is my account of our meeting, with Emil in full galloping flow:

"The stocky thin-haired man in the colonel's uniform would not wait for the lift in Prague on Sunday. He bounded up the three flights of stairs in the same impulsive way he seems to cover any distance once he is out of his car. At 44 Emil Zátopek still has the heart of an athlete.

"If his presence at the Olympics of 1948 gave particular pleasure to the British crowds then for Zátopek the Games were much more. Even, as he put it in his slow but fluent English, "a liberation of the spirit. After all those dark days of the war, the bombing, the killing and the starvation, the revival of the Olympics was as if the sun had come out.

"I went into the Olympic village and suddenly there were no more frontiers, no more barriers. Just the peoples meeting together. It was wonderfully warm. Men and women who had lost five years of the full life were back again, and there were the young ones, too.

"I never really saw London then, though I have done since. You know, I became so worried as I realised that I had a good chance in the 10,000 metres. I would say to myself again and again, 'Oh dear, there is Heino, of Finland, and all the others. Maybe I can win, but maybe I cannot'. Of course, to your public I was not a name until after my 10,000 metres victory.

"Then, perhaps, they took me to their hearts a little when I ran that incredibly stupid tactical 5000 metres race against Reiff, of Belgium. It was all so silly. Suddenly I was saying, 'Here is the last lap and maybe I can win'. But I had been too stupid. The crowd at London cheered for me, but when I got back to Czechoslovakia they asked, 'How could you be so stupid? How did it happen? '

"Everyone can make mistakes, and I often remember Chris Chataway in the 5000 metres at the 1954 European Championships. It is true that I slowed down the others, including him, when Kuts, the Russian, went far ahead. It was not very sporting of me, but then I was against Chataway because he would not do any leading. Afterwards they told me he said he had backed the wrong horse. I said that we were there not to back horses but to run against men!

"Perhaps what I remember best at London in 1948 is the opening ceremony. I wanted to see it, but I was told to rest and not tire myself in the hot sun. But I crept in at the back of our delegation and it was only much later in Wembley that our leaders saw me and began to mutter about lack of discipline. But by then it was all beginning - the march, you know - and I whispered back, 'The King is looking at us. How can I go off now?'

"Then I married Dana, another champion, and soon it was Helsinki and 1952. By then I was well known, and I have to smile as I remember the respect that I got from the other runners. When I went to the start of the 10,000 metres the others stood back and asked where Zátopek would like to stand, and when the gun went off they all fell into place behind me like schoolboys in a procession.

"Someone did a drawing of me after the Games, as if I were a railway engine and the others were carriages dropping off one by one as if in a goods yard. Shunting is, I think, the word in English. Well, my name is rather like our word for making fire, so perhaps that is how I was once called "the little stoker".

"But you see how easy is was for me then. The World of distance running was only Europe. We each knew our form and where we stood in our little World. Then I went to Tokyo and saw poor Ron Clarke attacked by everyone in the home straight - by the nobodies who had no respect for him, even though he was a minute faster. I felt so sorry for him. When I came home from Tokyo my wife said, 'Oh, Emil, it is very tough now. We were lucky to be champions when we were. Today I would have been afraid, for the whole World seems to run and throw'.

"But I would still try to be a champion if I were young again. You have something inside you which makes you always try, however hard it may seem, and I would be prepared to run 10,000 metres even in Mexico City, though I would not only make my legs strong I would try to do things with my breathing. It is right that the Games should go to Mexico, for the Olympics are the one true time in spite of all the records and the other meetings. At the Olympics you can say, 'These men are the best'. It is a big truth and everyone must have a chance to share.

"Now my wife coaches girls for field events and I am very busy in the army, planning physical training and making programmes. Now we get a house instead of a flat.

A POSTSCRIPT: BY NEIL ALLEN

"I have many happy memories and many many friends all over the World, but we must keep busy. We never stop running, and when the sun comes out at Olympic time it is all worthwhile. Give them all in England my regards and thank them for remembering."

Neil Allen was the athletics correspondent for "The Times" and then for the "Evening Standard" in London. His first journalistic assignments were as a junior reporter with the magazine, "Athletics World", edited by Norris & Ross McWhirter in the 1950s, and he has retained an infectious enthusiasm for the sport ever since. He now contributes to the "New York Times".

THE CAREER OF EMIL ZÁTOPEK IN FACTS & FIGURES

Compiled by Milan Skocovský & Stanislav Hrncír

Born 19.9.1922 in Koprivnice. Died 21.11.2000 in Prague, 1.82m/72kg

Progress of performances:

Club	Year	800m	1500m	5000m	10000m	Czech champ. 1500m	5000m	10000m
SK Bata Zlín	1941		4:20.9					
SK Bata Zlín	1942	2:03.2	4:13.9	16:25.0		4:13.9 (5)		
SK Bata Zlín	1943	1:59.0	4:01.0	15:26.6		4:07.2 (4)		
SK Bata Zlín	1944	2:01.1	3:59.5	14:54.9		4:02.8 (2)		
SK Bata Zlín	1945	2:04.9	4:01.4	14:50.8		4:05.8 (2)	14:50.8 (1)	
SK Bata Zlín	1946		3:57.6	14:25.8			14:48.0 (1)	
SK Bata Zlín	1947		3:52.8	14:08.2		Cross:	14:26.0 (1)	
Botostroj	1948			14:10.0	29:37.0	36:21.2 (1)	14:21.0 (1)	
ATK Praha	1949		3:57.0	14:10.2	29:21.2	38:15.2 (1)		
ATK Praha	1950			14:03.0	29:02.6		14:11.6 (1)	
ATK Praha	1951			14:11.6	29:29.8			
ATK Praha	1952			14:06.4	29:17.0	32:34.0 (1)	14:17.6 (1)	30:28.4 (1)
ÚDA Praha	1953			14:03.0	29:01.6		14:11.4 (1)	30:53.6 (1)
ÚDA Praha	1954		4:05.0	13:57.0	28:54.2	31:12.0 (1)	14:24.8 (1)	
ÚDA Praha	1955			14:04.0	29:25.6	30:55.4 (1)		
ÚDA Praha	1956			14:14.8	29:33.4	34:15.2 (2)		
Dukla Praha	1957			14:06.4	29:25.8			29:45.2 (2)
Dukla Praha	1958			15:13.0	31:13.0			

Olympic Games:

1948	5000 m	14:34.4 (2) h2	14:17.8 (2) 10,000m	29:59.6 (1)	
1952	5000 m	14:26.0 (3) h3	14:06.6 (1) 10,000m	29:17.0 (1)	Mar 2:23:03.2 (1)
1956					Mar 2:29:34.0 (6)

European Championships:

1946	5000m	14:25.8 (5)		
1950	5000m	14:56.0 (1) hl	14:03.0 (1) 10,000m	29:12.0 (1)
1954	5000m	14:36.2 (5) h2	14:10.2 (3) 10,000m	28:58.0 (1)

Czech records [*=World records]:

2000m:	3000m:	5000m:
5:33.4 Prague 01.10.44	8:34.8 Zlín 16.09.44	14:54.9 Zlín 23.09.44
5:30.4 Prague 11.07.46	8:33.4 Prague 01.07.45	14:50.8 Prague 18.08.45
5:27.4 Prague 23.07.47	8:33.2 Zlín 29.06.46	14:36.6 Prague 10.06.46
5:20.6 Bratislava 21.08.47	8:26.8 Prague 04.07.46	14:25.8 Oslo 23.08.46
	8:21.0 Brno 28.07.46	14:08.2 Prague 25.06.47
	8:13.6 Zlín 08.06.47	14:06.2 Helsinki 02.08.50
	8:12.8 Prague 23.07.47	14:03.0 Brussels 26.08.50
	8:08.8 Brno 18.08.47	14:03.0 Bucharest 05.08.53
	8:07.8 Zlín 11.06.48	13:57.2 *Paris 30.05.54
		13:57.0 Stockholm 03.09.54

THE CAREER OF EMIL ZÁTOPEK IN FACTS & FIGURES

3 miles:
13:31.2 Stockholm 03.09.54

6 miles:
28:30.2 Bucharest 09.08.53
28:08.4*St.Boleslav 01.11.53
27:59.2*Brussels 01.06.54

10,000m:
30:28.4 Budapest 29.05.48
29:37.0 Prague 17.06.48
29:28.2*Ostrava 11.06.49
29:21.2*Ostrava 22.10.49
29:02.6*Turku 04.08.50
29:01.6* St.Boleslav 01.11.53
28:54.2* Brussels 01.06.54

10 miles:
49:32.6 Prague 15.09.51
48:12.0* St.Boleslav 29.09.51

20,000m:
1:01:15.8* Prague 15.09.51
59:51.8* St.Boleslav 29.09.51

15 miles:
1:16:26.4* St.Boleslav 26.10.52
1:14:01.0* Celákovice 29.10.55

25,000m:
1:19:11.8* St.Boleslav 26.10.52
1:16:36.4* Celákovice 29.10.55

30,000m:
1:35:23.8* St.Boleslav 26.10.52

1 hour:
19,558m* Prague 15.09.51
20,052m* St.Boleslav 29.09.51

4x1500m relay:
17:01.6 Prague	23.08.42
16:59.4 Zlín	19.09.43
16:40.2 Zlín	22.08.48
16:22.8 Gottwaldov	30.07.50
16:16.8 Olomouc	21.09.52
15:45.4 Partizánske	14.10.52

Year-by-Year World rankings:

Year	5000m	10,000m
1944	5000m - 14:54.9 (30)	
1945	5000m - 14:50.8 (23)	
1946	5000m - 14:25.8 (5)	
1947	5000m - 14:08.2 (1)	
1948	5000m - 14:10.0 (1)	10,000m - 29:37.0 (1)
1949	5000m - 14:10.2 (1)	10,000m - 29:21.2 (1)
1950	5000m - 14:03.0 (1)	10,000m - 29:02.6 (1)
1951	5000m - 14:11.6 (2)	10,000m - 29:29.8 (1)
1952	5000m - 14:06.4 (1)	10,000m - 29:17.0 (1)
1953	5000m - 14:03.0 (5)	10.000m - 29:01.6 (1)
1954	5000m - 13:57.0 (3)	10,000m - 28:54.2 (1)
1955	5000m - 14:04.0 (11=)	10,000m - 29:25.6 (8)
1956	5000m - 14:14.8 (49=)	10,000m - 29:33.4 (17)
1957	5000m - 14:06.4 (24)	10,000m - 29:25.8 (11)

Zátopek's races at 5000 metres:

141 races, 120 wins, 21 defeats (including three in heats)

Time		Place	Date	Notes
16:25.0	(1)	Zlín	19.09.42	Zlín later Gottwaldov, now Zlín
15:26.6	(1)	Zlín	16.10.43	2 Kubát 16:42.0, 3 Zdráhal 16:56.0
15:38.7	(2)	Zlín	26.06.44	1 Haluza 15:35.6, 3 Vanak 16:13.3
14:54.9 NR	(1)	Zlín	23.09.44	2 Roudný 16:41.0, 3 Sobotka 17:59.2
14:50.8 NR NCh	(1)	Prague	18.08.45	2 Diringer 16:02.0, 3 Gálffy 16:05.4
15.08.0	(1)	Brno	02.09.45	2 Kosour 16:04.9
15:14.8	(1)	Ostrava	16.09.45	2 Diringer 15:47.0, 3 Kosour 16:03.6
14:36.6 NR	(1)	Prague	10.06.46	2 Hercík 15:56.0, 3 Jílek 16:00.6
14:48.0 NCh	(1)	Prague	10.08.46	2 Steiner 15:48.4, 3 Hercík 15:50.4
14:25.8 NR ECh	(5)	Oslo	23.08.46	1 Wooderson 14:08.6, 2 Slijkhuis 14:14.0

ZÁ-TO-PEK! ZÁ-TO-PEK! ZÁ-TO-PEK!

3 Nyberg 14:23.2, 4 Heino 14:24.4, 6 Reiff 14:45.8

Time	Pl	City	Date	Results
14:31.0	(1)	Berlin	08.09.46	
14:51.0	(1)	Plzen	22.09.46	2 Hercík 15:45.0, 3 Vlášek 16:33.0
15:05.1	(1)	Olomouc	05.10.46	2 Macký 16:30.4, 3 Šalé 16:55.0
14:08.2 NR	(1)	Prague	25.06.47	2 Nyberg 14:59.4, 3 Koskela 15:05.6
14:15.2	(1)	Helsinki	30.06.47	2 Heino 14:15.4, 3 Järvinen 14.39.8
14:38.4 vHOL	(1)	Enschede	12.07.47	2 Slijkhuis 15:01.8, 3 Lataster 15:19.6
14:17.2 vITA	(1)	Prague	19.07.47	2 G.Nocco 15:14.8, 3 Beviacqua 15:16.6
14:26.0 NCh	(1)	Prague	02.08.47	2 Hercík 15:39.8, 3 Bakaliar 15:40.0
14:15.0 vFRA	(1)	Prague	16.08.47	2 Mimoun 15:12.8, 3 Pouzieux 15:17.0
14:20.8	(1)	Paris (Col)	31.08.47	2 Joly 15.12.4, 3 Barbaud 15:15.4
14:20.6	(1)	Ostrava	07.09.47	2 Löfgren 15:14.2, 3 Stelbaský 15:59.8
14:19.8	(1)	Plzen	14.09.47	2 Rickardsson 15:40.8, 3 Šourek 16:01.2
14:21.5	(1)	Warsaw	07.10.47	2 Kielas 15:32.0, 3 Zwonowski 15:53.4
14:22.5	(1)	Gdansk	09.10.47	2 Kielas 15:16.5, 3 Bonicki 15:16.9
14:20.0	(1)	Katowice	12.10.47	2 Junzak 15:54.2, 3 J.Štrup 16:22.2
14:29.6	(1)	Zlín	09.05.48	2 Zelenka 16:31.5, 3 Meliš 18:32.5
14:20.0 Prague-Belgrade	(1)	Prague	05.06.48	2 Stefanovic 15:24.4, 3 Mihalic 15:26.6
14:10.0 vHOL/HUN	(1)	Prague	22.06.48	2 Szilágyi 14:53.0, 3 Szegedi 14:53.0, Slijkhuis DNF
14:21.0 NCh	(1)	Prague	30.06.48	2 Švajgr 15:20.8, 3 Dolenský 15:41.4
14:34.4 OG	(2)h2	London	31.07.48	1 Ahldén 14:34.2, 3 Mäkelä 14:45.8
14:17.8 OG	(2)	London	02.08.48	1 Reiff 14:17.6, 3 Slijkuis 14:26.8, 4 Ahldén 14:28.6, 5 Albertsson 14:39.0, 6 Stone 14:39.4
14:21.4	(1)	Prague	18.08.48	2 Albertsson 14:44.2, 3 Wilt 14:44.6
14:28.4 vFRA	(1)	Paris	05.09.48	2 Mimoun 15:09.2, 3 Vernier 15:45.6
14:21.2 vBEL	(2)	Prague	12.09.48	1 Reiff 14:19.0, 3 Herman 15:51.2
14:30.2 vITA	(1)	Bologna	03.10.48	2 G.Nocco 15:11.0, 3 Švajgr 15:19.8
14:22.2	(1)	Milan	10.10.48	2 G.Nocco 15:13.8, Peliccoli 15:16.4
14:16.8	(1)	Prague	13.10.48	2 Ahldén 14:56.0, 3 Roudný 15:04.8
14:23.6	(1)	Prague	04.05.49	2 Zelenka 15:30.0, 3 Liška 15:51.4
14:10.2	(1)	Warsaw	09.05.49	2 Szilágyi 15:07.8, 3 Kielas 15:35.0
14:32.2	(1)	Prague	21.05.49	2 Novák 15:53.6, 3 Šourek 16:11.8
14:14.4	(1)	Stockholm	15.06.49	2 Mäkelä 14:42.0, 3 Durkfeld 14:44.0
14:20.0	(1)	Helsinki	13.07.49	2 Koskela 14:20.8, 3 Mäkelä 14:27.2
14:13.2	(1)	Turku	15.07.49	2 Koskela 14:13.2, 3 Mäkelä 14:46.6
14:29.0 vUSSR	(1)	Moscow	25.07.49	2 Kazantsev 14:30.0, 3 Popov 14:30.8
14:39.6	(1)	Brno	06.08.49	2 Kuda 15:45.0, 3 Zanta 15:46.0
14:27.4	(1)	Plzen	10.08.49	2 Klomínek 15:21.5, Koller 16:03.8
14:35.2 vHUN//ITA	(1)	Budapest	29.08.49	2 Szilágyi 15:07.8, 3 Bacsfálvi 15:09.0
14:24.0	(1)	Bucharest	10.09.49	2 Bacsfálvi 14:54.4, 3 Radu 15:42.6
14:40.6 Prague-Warsaw	(1)	Prague	25.09.49	2 Kielas 15:36.8, 3 Klomínek 15:37.6
14:44.2	(1)	Gottwaldov	21.05.50	2 Šourek 15:56.6, 3 Zelenka 16:24.0
14:23.4	(1)	Berlin	29.05.50	
14:26.2	(1)	Prague	03.06.50	2 Diringer 15:43.6, 3 Hovorka 16:51.2
14:17.2	(1)	Prague	10.06.50	2 Švajgr 14:54.8, Szegedi 15:08.8
14:31.0	(1)	Brno	16.06.50	2 Šourek 15:45, Skládaný 16.00.04
14:31.0 vPOL	(1)	Warsaw	02.07.50	2 Kielas 15:25.8, 3 Šourek 15:27.0
14:28.6 vHUN	(1)	Bratislava	09.07.50	2 Švajgr 14:59.4, 3 Szegedi 15:24.8
14:22.6	(1)	Brno	14.07.50	2 Švajgr 15:04.6, 3 Liška 15:15.8
14:06.2 NR	(1)	Helsinki	02.08.50	2 Salonen 14:43.0, 3 Nieminen
14:18.8	(1)	Tampere	07.08.50	2 Salonen 14:51.2, Puolakka
14:11.6 NCh	(1)	Bratislava	12.08.50	2 Švajgr 15:00.2, 3 Bacigál 15:06.2
14:56.0 ECh	(1)h1	Brussels	24.08.50	2 Mäkelä 14:56.2, 3 Theys 15:03.0
14:03.0 NR ECh	(1)	Brussels	26.08.50	2 Mimoun 14:26.0, 3 Reiff 14:26.2, 4 Mäkelä 14:30.8, 5 Posti 14:40.8, 6 Theys 14:42.4
14:05.2 vFIN	(1)	Prague	31.08.50	2 Mäkelä 14:52.6, 3 Posti 14:52.6
14:39.4	(1)	Bucharest	09.09.50	2 Spasov 15:27.4, 3 Levänen 15:33.6

THE CAREER OF EMIL ZÁTOPEK IN FACTS & FIGURES

Time		Place	Date	Others
14:24.2	(1)	Plzen	16.09.50	2 Švajgr 15:11.4, 3 Šourek 15:24.6
14:16.2	(1)	Prague	08.10.50	2 Bílý 15:11.2, 3 Šourek 15:39.2
14:21.4	(1)	Dresden	12.10.50	2 Bartolomeo
14:32.4	(1)	Erfurt	14.10.50	2 Witerhangen 15:39.2, 3 Tehn
14:21.4 vUSSR	(1)	Prague	29.10.50	2 Švajgr 14:46.4, 3 Kazantsev 14:48.4
15:00.8	(1)	Zlín	20.05.51	2 Bacigál 15:32.3, 3 Šourek 15:39.5
14:58.4	(1)	Gottwaldov	10.06.51	2 Tomis
14:56.0	(1)	Jablonec	16.06.51	2 Tomis 15:54.6
15:02.2	(1)	Lomnice n.P.	17.06.51	2 Tomis 16:09.0
14:15.0	(1)	Prague	24.06.51	2 Švajgr 15.00.0, 3 Bacigál 15.02.8
14:28.2	(1)	Ostrava	14.07.51	2 Švajgr 14:48.8
14:11.6	(1)	Berlin	18.08.51	2 Bacigál 14:51.6
14:30.2 vHUN	(1)	Budapest	26.08.51	2 Pénzes 14:51.0, 3 Bacigál 14:54.0
14:23.2	(1)	Prague	09.09.51	2 Tomis 15:06.8, 3 Harazim 15:37.6
14:16.4	(1)	Prague	07.10.51	2 Roudný 15:03.3, 3 Tomis 15:04.6
14:39.8	(1)	Chodov	21.10.51	
14:32.6	(1)	Prostejov	28.10.51	2 Brandýs 16:09.9
14:46.4	(1)	Prague	21.05.52	2 Šantrucek 15:10.4
14:33.8	(1)	Leipzig	01.06.52	2 Béres 14:54.0, 3 Graj 14:58.2
14:22.0	(3)	Kiev	11.06.52	1 Kazantsev 14:13.2, 2 Popov 14:16.0
14:17.6 NCh	(1)	Prague	27.06.52	2 Švajgr 14:39.4, 3 Roudný 15:09.0
14:26.0 OG	(3)h3	Helsinki	22.07.52	1 Anufriyev 14:23.6, 2 Albertsson 14:26.0
14:06.6 OG	(1)	Helsinki	24.07.52	2 Mimoun 14:07.4, 3 Schade 14:08.6, 4 Pirie 14:18.0, 5 Chataway 14:18.0, 6 Perry 14:23.6
14:33.4	(1)	Prague	14.08.52	2 Tomis 15:15.2, 3 Uzsoki 15:27.6
14:17.8	(1)	Gottwaldov	28.08.52	2 Šourek 15:17.3, 3 Macky 15:58.0
14:22.6	(1)	Brno	30.08.52	2 Tomis 14:55.8, 3 Škuta 16:32.8
14:19.6	(1)	Znojmo	02.09.52	2 Švajgr 14:32.2, 3 Tomis 15:14.4
14:20.6	(1)	St.Boleslav	06.09.52	2 Cevona 14:51.8, 3 Havenstein 15:10.4
14:19.4	(1)	Olomouc	13.09.52	2 Švajgr 14:46.8
14:22.9	(1)	Ústí nad Labem	17.09.52	2 Švajgr 14:39.0, 3 Koller 15:26.0
14:19.8	(1)	Warsaw	27.09.52	2 Krzyszkowiak 14:39.6, 3 Olesinski 15:19.8
14:06.4	(1)	Opava	04.10.52	2 Švajgr 15:09.4, 3 Roudný 15:10.6
14:33.0	(1)	Prague	24.05.53	2 Tomis 15:19.8, 3 Šourek 15:24.8
14:26.8	(1)	Jablonec	06.06.53	2 Koubek 15:12.0, 3 Klominek 15:17.0
14:22.6	(1)	Prague	13.06.53	2 Koubek 15:02.8, Kocev 16:06.8
14:28.6 vHUN	(1)	Prague	11.07.53	2 Béres 14:50.8, 3 Szabó 14:50.8
14:11.4 NCh	(1)	Prague	24.07.53	2 Košilka 15:04.4, 3 Koller 15:06.2
14:03.0	(1)	Bucharest	05.08.53	2 Kuts 14:04.0, 3 Kovács 14:04.2, 4 Anufriyev 14:15.0, 5 Chromik 14:21.6, 6 Szabó 14:38.8
14:33.2	(1)	Sofia	27.09.53	2 Asenov 16:38.8, 3 Stoyev 17:18.0
14:26.6	(1)	Warsaw	11.10.53	2 Tábori 14:42.8, 3 Mankowski 14:44.8
14:09.0	(1)	Prague	17.10.53	2 Kovács 14:14.0, 3 Roudný 15:03.6
14:34.8	(-)	St Boleslav	01.11.53	Made during 10,000m race
14:04.0	(1)	St.Boleslav	14.05.54	2 Ullsperger 14:33.6, 3 Koubek 14:35.8
14:19.2	(1)	Kladno	16.05.54	2 Ullsperger 14:46.8, 3 Tomis 14:59.6
13:57.2 WR	(1)	Paris (Col)	30.05.54	2 Stritof 14:43.2, 3 Pavlovic 14:45.6
14:17.8	(1)	Prague	20.06.54	2 Ullsperger 14:33.0, 3 Koubek 14:47.0
14:18.2 vHUN	(1)	Budapest	04.07.54	2 Szabó 14:18.4, 3 Tábori 14:49,2
14:24.8 NCh	(1)	Ostrava	06.08.54	2 Koubek 14:57.0, 3 Švajgr 15:03.2
14:36.2 ECh	(5)h2	Berne	26.08.54	1 Kuts 14:18.8, 2 Schade 14:23.8, 3 Hanswijck 14:29.2, 4 Julin 14:36.2, 6 Page 14:37.4
14:10.2 ECh	(3)	Berne	29.08.54	1 Kuts 13:56.6 WR, 2 Chataway 14:08.8, 4 Okorokov 14:20.0, 5 Hanswijck 14:25.6, 6 Herman 14:31.4
13:57.0 NR	(1)	Stockholm	03.09.54	2 T.Nilsson 14:31.8, 3 Andersson 14:32.0
14:04.6	(1)	Brno	18.09.54	2 Šantrucek 14:47.4, 3 Koller 15:21.4

155

ZÁ-TO-PEK! ZÁ-TO-PEK! ZÁ-TO-PEK!

14:24.6 vSWE	(1)	Prague	01.10.54	2 Källevagh14:33.4, 3 Ullsperger 14:34.6
14:19.0 vUSSR	(2)	Prague	23.10.54	1 Kuts 13:51.2 WR, 3 Ullsperger 14:25.2, 4 Okorokov 14:55.2
14:19.6	(2)	Brno	28.05.55	1 Ullsperger 14:10.0, 3 Koller 14:55.0
14:11.8	(2)	Prague	09.06.55	1 Ullsperger 14:09.8, 3 Konrad 14:23.6
14:49.6	(5)	Belgrade	16.06.55	1 Konrad 14:14.0, 2 Stritof 14:18.6, 3 Kopinar 14:27.0, 4 Maynard 14:35.0
14:31.2	(1)	Karlsruhe	17.07.55	2 Konrad 14:53.4, 3 Porbadnik 14:59.6
14:17.2	(1)	Nüremburg	18.07.55	2 Laufer 14:25.0, 3 Suárez 14:26.2
14:36.4	(1)	Prague	21.07.55	2 Koller 14:44.8, 3 Tomis 14:45.2
14:11.4	(6)	Warsaw	06.08.55	1 Chromik 13:55.2, 2 Iharos 13:56.6, 3 Kovács 13:57.6, 4 Szabó 14:00.6, 5 Krzyszkowiak 14:05.8
14:24.4 vFRA	(1)	Prague	24.08.55	2 Šantrucek 14:35.4, Labidi 14:40.4
14:07.6 vPOL	(1)	Brno	30.08.55	2 Krzyszkowiak 14:15.8, 3 Tomis 14:22.6
14:04.0 vGB	(2)	Prague	14.09.55	1 Pirie 14:03.8, 3 K. Norris 14:04.0
14:24.2	(2)	Manchester	15.10.55	1 Pirie 14:19.0, 3 Sando 14:28.0
14:19.6	(1)	Bratislava	05.06.56	2 Tomis 14:19.6, 3 Hec 15:02.4
14:14.8	(5)	Prague	16.06.56	1 Szabó 14:07.2, 2 Kovács 14:08.6, 3 Gräf 14:08.6, 4 Tomis 14:14.0, 6 Rudolf 14:15.2
15:18.6	(1)	Kladno	26.08.56	
14:22.0	(1)	Plzen	26.05.57	2 Rudolf 14:38.4, 3 Tomis 14:40.2
14:12.0	(3)	Prague	15.06.57	1 Gräf 14:06.2, 2 Bolotnikov 14:10.0, 4 Jurek 14:17.4
14:06.4	(3)	Oslo	15.07.57	1 Jurek 14:00.4, 2 Larsen 14:03.8
14:08.0	(2)	Stockholm	19.07.57	1 Jurek 13:59.6, 3 Veselý 14:17.2
14:36.2	(1)	Athens	14.08.57	2 Papavassiliou 14:41.6, Tomis 15:10.2
14:35.5	(4)	Berlin	25.08.57	1 Havenstein 14:19.4, 2 Mitschke 14:19.8, 3 Hönicke 14:20.4
14:18,2	(1)	Odessa	18.10.57	2 Desyatchikov 14:24.2, 3 Rzhishchin 14:30.4
14:23.0	(1)	Prague	25.10.57	2 Kantorek 14:35.0
14:18.4	(1)	Prague	28.10.57	
15:13.0			1958	

Zátopek's races at 10,000 metres:

62 races, 54 wins, eight defeats

30:28.4 NR	(1)	Budapest	29.05.48	2 Szilágyi 30:48.4, 3 Szegedi 31:35.2
29:37.0 NR	(1)	Prague	17.06.48	2 Jílek 35:28.4, 3 Weisshäutel 35:54.4
29:59.6 OG	(1)	London	30.07.48	2 Mimoun 30:47.4, 3 Albertsson 30:53.6, 4 Stokken 30:58.6, 5 Dennolf 31:05.6, 6 Everaert 31:07.8
30:03.6	(1)	Bucharest	26.09.48	2 Szilágyi 31:01.0, 3 Szegedi 31:31.8
30:09.8 vITA	(1)	Bologna	02.10.48	2 Panico 32:46.8, 3 Malachina 33:19.6,
29:28.2 WR	(1)	Ostrava	11.06.49	2 Zanta 32:25.8, 3 Wilham 33:02.0
29:49.6 vRUM	(1)	Ostrava	18.06.49	2 Ionita 32:06.6, 3 Cristea 32:07.0
29:58.4 vFIN	(1)	Helsinki	12.07.49	2 Heino 30:12.2, 3 Könönen 30:46.4
30:11.2	(1)	Moscow	28.07.49	2 Kazantsev 31:07.4, 3 Popov 31:11.2
30:14.0	(1)	Trebíc	20.08.49	2 Novák 32:47.0, 3 Zanta 33:25.4
30:00.4 vHUN	(1)	Budapest	30.08.49	2 Csordás 31:41.0, 3 Jészenszky 32:08.0
30:30.8 vBUL	(1)	Sofia	03.09.49	2 Grigorov 33:04.6, 3 Augustin 33:07.0
30:01.2	(1)	Bucharest	11.09.49	2 Szilágyi 31:31.0, 3 Banhalmi 31:49.0
29:38.2	(1)	Ostrava	17.09.49	2 Novák 32:29.2, 3 Augustin 33:04.8
30:03.0	(1)	Prague	29.09.49	2= Zanta & Tomis 32:35.0
29:21.2 WR	(1)	Ostrava	22.10.49	2 Klomínek 32:24.2, 3 Novák 32:26.8
29:54.2 vHUN	(1)	Bratislava	08.07.50	2 Szilágyi 32:05.6, 3 Šourek 32:06.6
29:02.6 WR	(1)	Turku	04.08.50	2 Ukkonen 31:56.8, 3 Levänen 32:51.0
29:12.0 ECh	(1)	Brussels	23.08.50	2 Mimoun 30:21.0, 3 Koskela 30:30.8, 4 Aaron

THE CAREER OF EMIL ZÁTOPEK IN FACTS & FIGURES

30:31.6, 5 Popov 30:34.4, 6 Stokken 30:44.8

Mark	(Pos)	Place	Date	Details
29:54.6 vFIN	(1)	Prague	30.08.50	2 Salonen 31:23.4, 3 Koskela 31:55.2
29:35.0	(1)	Trebíc	02.09.50	2 Salonen 31:28.0, 3 Šourek 32:34.8
30:02.4	(1)	Bucharest	11.09.50	2 Dinu 32:42.6, 3 Ionita 32:54.6
29:53.2 vUSSR	(1)	Prague	30.10.50	2 Vanin 31:40.8, 3 Semyonov 32:16.2
30:01.4 vHUN	(1)	Budapest	25.08.51	2 Juhász 32:28.2, 3 Liška 32:34.2
29:29.8	(1)	Trebíc	01.09.51	2 Liška 32:15.4, 3 Šourek 32:16.4
30:01.8	(1)	Prague	08.09.51	2 Šourek 33.08.4, 3 Kalfus 37:55.4
31:05.6	(-)	Prague	15.09.51	made during 20,000m race
30:10.4	(-)	Prague	15.09.51	2nd 10,000m in 20,000m race
29:53.4	(-)	St.Boleslav	29.09.51	made during 20,000m race
29:58.4	(-)	St.Boleslav	29.09.51	2nd 10,000 m in 20,000 m race
30:08.8	(1)	Leipzig	30.05.52	2 Juhász 30:37.8, 3 Syring 32:41.8
29:26.0	(1)	Kiev	12.06.52	2 Anufriyev 29:31.4, 3 Semyonov 30:11.0
30:28.4 NCh	(1)	Prague	29.06.52	2 Švajgr 31:02.6, 3 Tomis 32:13.8
29:17.0 OG	(1)	Helsinki	20.07.52	2 Mimoun 29:32.8, 3 Anufriyev 29:48.2, 4 Posti 29:51.4, 5 Sando 29:51.8, 6 Nyström 29:54.8, 7 Pirie 30:04.2
30:58.6	(1)	Prague	15.08.52	2 Šourek 32:10.4, 3 Kovács 33:02.8
29:34.0	(1)	Warsaw	28.09.52	2 Szwargot 31:45.8, 3 Koller 31:59.0
31:43.6	(-)	St.Boleslav	26.10.52	1st 10,000 m in 30,000m race
31:32.6	(-)	St.Boleslav	26.10.52	2nd 10,000 m in 30,000 m race
32:08.6	(-)	St.Boleslav	26.10.52	3rd 10,000 m in 30,000m race
29:48.6 vHUN	(1)	Prague	12.07.53	2 Kovács 30:15.6, 3 Juhász 30:57.6
30:53.6 NCh	(1)	Prague	26.07.53	2 Šourek 32:30.4, 3 Šantrucek 32:58.8
29:25.8	(1)	Bucharest	09.08.53	2 Kuts 29:41.4, 3 Anufriyev 30:03.4
29:01.6 WR	(1)	St.Boleslav	01.11.53	2 Tomis 31:12.2, 3 Liška 31:12.4
30:09.0	(1)	Sao Paulo	06.01.54	2 Eberlein 31:32.4, 3 Suarez 32:13.0
28:54.2 WR	(1)	Brussels	01.06.54	2 van de Wattyne 30:50.0, 3 Cromphout
29:09.8 vHUN	(2)	Budapest	03.07.54	1 Kovács 29:09.0, 3 Juhász 30:02.2
30:08.0	(1)	Prague	31.07.54	2 Novák 33:16.4, 3 Šimonovic 33:16.6
28:58.0 ECh	(1)	Berne	25.08.54	2 Kovács 29:25.8, 3 Sando 29:27.6, 4 Schade 29:32.8, 5 Mihalic 29:59.6, 6 Driver 30:03.6
29:34.8 vSWE	(1)	Prague	02.10.54	2 Šantrucek 30:39.2, 3 Söderberg 30:39.4
29:20.8 vUSSR	(1)	Prague	24.10.54	2 Anufriyev 30:18.8, 3 Šantrucek 30:22.6
29:33.0	(1)	St.Boleslav	14.05.55	2 Šantrucek 30:14.8, 3 Tomis 31:10.2
29:54.0	(1)	Prague	29.06.55	2 Rudolf 30:23.4, 3 Hercík 31:36.0
29:34.4	(1)	Warsaw	02.08.55	2 Basalayev 29:50.0, 3 Ozog 29:51.8
29:58.0 vPOL	(1)	Brno	31.08.55	2 Ozog 30:32.8, 3 Šantrucek 30:39.6
29:25.6 vGB	(1)	Prague	15.09.55	2 Pirie 29:54.0, 3 Sando 30:00.8
29:46,4 vHUN	(3)	Bratislava	24.09.55	1 Kovács 29:02.6, 2 Szabó 29:31.2
29:28.6 Prague-London	(3)	London	12.10.55	1 Pirie 29:19.0, 2 K. Norris 29:21.4
30:24.2	(-)	Celákovice	29.10.55	1st 10,000m in 25,000m race
30:43.2	(-)	Celákovice	29.10.55	2nd 10,000m in 25,000m race
(30:52,0)	(-)	Celákovice	29.10.55	(15,000m to 25,000 m)
29:33.4	(1)	Prague	07.10.56	2 Tomis 29:42.6, 3 Ozog 29:44.6
30:00.0 vPOL	(1)	Craców	30.06.57	2 Kantorek 30:19.6, 3 Plonka 30:20.2
30:04.2	(6)	Moscow	30.07.57	1.Bolotnikov 29:14.6, 2.Lawrence 29:16.4, 3 Chernyavskiy 29:36.0, 4 Janke 29:52.6, 5 Desyatchikov 29:53.0
30:31.0	(1)	Athens	15.08.57	2 Tomis 31:37.0
29:45.2 NCh	(2)	Prague	23.08.57	1 Ullsperger 29:44.4, 3 Kantorek 30:18.8
30:06.4	(2)	Solingen	07.09.57	1 Schade 29:37.0
29:47.0 vHUN	(2)	Prague	14.09.57	1 Szabó 29:46.4, 3 Ullsperger 30:10.8
29:28.0 vGFR	(1)	Berlin	22.09.57	2 Schade 29:29.2, 3 Konrad 30:19.2
29:29.4	(1)	Prague	05.10.57	2 Tomis 30:27.2, 3 Cesal 30:43.2
29:25.8 vGDR	(2)	Brno	12.10.57	1 Janke 29:21.2, 3 Kantorek 30:09.0

ZÁ-TO-PEK! ZÁ-TO-PEK! ZÁ-TO-PEK!

29:38.8   (1)   Odessa   20.10.57   2 Desyatchikov 29:58.2, 3 Ullsperger 30:39.4
31:13.0   Beijing   26.10.58

Zátopek's races at 3000 metres:

54 races, 46 wins, eight defeats

9:12.0	(2)	Zlín	18.07.42	1. Haluza 9:07.6,
8:56.0	(-)	Zlín	16.10.43	made during 5000m race
8:57.1	(1)	Zlín	23.10.43	2 Aigl 9:41.8, 3 Zdráhal 9:47.4
8:34.8 NR	(1)	Zlín	16.09.44	2 Roudný 9:24.4, 3 Kubát 9:47.0
8:45.2	(1)	Zlín	17.06.45	2 Roudný 9:21.5, 3 Konecný 9:55.0
8:33.4 NR	(1)	Prague	01.07.45	2 Roudný 9:01.4, 3 Ajgl 9:04.8
8:48.2	(1)	Bratislava	09.05.46	2 Muschik 9:24.1, 3 Retzel 9:25.0
8:33.2 NR	(1)	Zlín	29.06.46	2 Zelenka 9:36.2, 3 Petr 9:52.5
8:26.8. NR	(2)	Prague	04.07.46	1 Sundin 8:25.6, 3 Steiner 9:02.2
8:27.8	(1)	Ostrava	26.07.46	2 Steiner 8:53.4, 3 Roudný 8:53.8
8:21.0 NR	(2)	Brno	28.07.46	1 Slijkhuis 8:15.5, 3 Roudný 9:10.9
8:35.8	(1)	Semily	15.09.46	2 Hercík 9:22.0
8:34.0	(1)	Zlín	28.09.46	2 Hercík 8:54.6, 3 Roudný 8:55.1
8:13.6 NR	(1)	Zlín	08.06.47	2 Zelenka 9:32.0, 3 Augustin 9:38.8
8:12.8 NR	(2)	Prague	23.07.47	1 Slijkhuis 8:10.0, 3 Steiner 9:01.4
8:08.8 NR	(1)	Brno	18.08.47	2 Steiner 8:55.1, 3 Hovorka 9:21.6
8:12.2	(1)	Olomouc	10.09.47	2 Löfgren 8:37.4, 3 Rickardsson 8:57.8
8:14.6 vBEL	(2)	Brussels	20.09.47	1 Reiff 8:14.2, 3 van de Wattyne 8:47.5
8:25.0	(1)	Tirlemont	21.09.47	
8:18.8	(1)	Zlín	28.09.47	2 Hercík 8:54.0, 3 Bakaliar 8:54.6
8:25.2	(1)	Warsaw	05.10.47	2 Ostolski
8:14.7	(1)	Algiers	25.12.47	2 Vernier 8:36.5, 3 Heirendt 8:47.0
8:22.2	(1)	Prague	12.05.48	2 Švajgr 9:03.4, 3 Tomis 9:19.4
8:18.0	(1)	Bratislava	16.05.48	2 Zelenka, 3 Augustin 9:12.2
8:14.4	(1)	St.Boleslav	09.06.48	2 Cevona 8:32.8, 3 Segedin 8:51.8
8:07.8 NR	(1)	Zlín	11.06.48	2 Stefanovic 8:45.4, 3 Mihalic 8:46.0
				During 4000m race (1) 11:14.2
8:24.0	(1)	Budejovice	14.07.48	2 Rudolf 9:04.9, 3 Nemec 9:53.0
8:18.8	(1)	Olomouc	17.07.48	2 Hrdlicka 8:53.4, Kantorek 9:05.4
8:35.2	(1)	Ostende	08.08.48	2 Vernier 9:11.5, 3 Everaert
8:18.0	(1)	Brussels	13.08.48	2 Thompson 8:35.6, Herman 8:35.8
8:16.0	(3)	Amsterdam	15.08.48	1 Ahldén 8:09.6, 2 Slijkhuis 8:10.2
8:16.2	(1)	Brno	20.08.48	2 Mäkelä 8:37.8, 3 Roudný 8:50.4
8:36.2	(1)	Prague	27.03.49	2 Liška 9:08.8, 3 Štelbaský 9:08.8
8:27.2	(1)	Brno	15.05.49	2 Zuba 9:36.8, 3 Jeník 9:41.4
8:23.4	(1)	Košice	29.05.49	2 Garay 8:43.7, 3 Apró 8:45.0
8:25.8	(1)	Prešov	30.05.49	2 Augustin 9:01.2, 3 Bacigal 9:21.5
8:19.2	(1)	Pori	17.07.49	2 Koskela 8:19.4, 3 Taipale 8:29.4
8:44.5	(1)	Olomouc	14.08.49	2 Klomínek 8:59.8, 3 Brlica 8:59.8
8:33.8	(1)	Prostejov	14.08.49	2 Zanta 9:03.2, Klomínek 9:03.6
8:30.8	(1)	Sochi	28.04.50	
8:31.6	(1)	Prague	07.05.50	2 Liška 8:51.2, 2 Tešcák 8:53.6
8:29.6	(1)	Berlin	27.05.50	2 Görtl 9:15.8, Tees 9:16.6
8:17.6	(1)	Olomouc	17.06.50	2 Švajgr 8:30.6
8:16.8	(1)	Opava	24.06.50	2 Švajgr 8:21.2, 3 Liška 8:43.2
8:16.0	(1)	Prostejov	25.06.50	2 Švajgr 8:35.4
8:34.6	(1)	Pardubice	12.05.51	2 Roudný 8:55.4, 3 Šourek 8:57.0
8:41.2	(1)	Ustí n. Orlicí	13.05.51	2 Steiner 9:07.0, 3 Tomis
8:37.5	(1)	Svit	18.05.51	

158

8:17.6	(1)	Olomouc	02.06.51	2 Švajgr 8:25.6
8:33.4	(-)	Prague	24.06.51	made during 5000m race
8:30.4	(2)	Prague	11.07.51	1 Cevona 8:27.4, 3 Slavicek 8:36.0
8:32.4	(1)	Hradec		
		Králové	25.04.52	2 Tomis 8:51.4, 3 Peterek 8:52.2
8:44.4	(1)	Bratislava	26.05.52	2 Roudný 8:57.8
8:34.0	(-)	Olomouc	13.09.52	made during 5000m race
8:23.2	(-)	Opava	04.10.52	made during 5000m race
8:13.8	(2)	Opava	27.06.53	1 Jungwirth 8:12.2, 3 Švajgr 8:35.8
8:24.4	(1)	Sofia	25.09.53	2 Danilov 9:05.0, 3 Asenov 9:27.4
8:19.0	(-)	Stockholm	03.09.54	made during 5000m race
8:26.8	(-)	Prague	14.09.55	made during 5000m race
8:18.4	(1)	Ostrava	10.10.57	2 Grodotzki 8:24.4, 3 Hlušmanjuk 8:54.0

N.B. Zátopek also ran one race at 400m (in 1943), 16 at 800m (1942-45), seven at 1000m (1942-46) and eight at 2000m (1944-47). His best times in these events were: 56.2, 1:59.0, 2:34.6, 3:52.8 and 5:20.5

BY THE SAME AUTHOR

Honour of Empire, Glory of Sport:
The History of Athletics at the Commonwealth Games
(The Parrs Wood Press 2000)

The Iron In His Soul:
Bill Roberts & Manchester's Sporting Heritage
(The Parrs Wood Press 2002)

The Commonwealth Games:
The History of all the Sports
(The Parrs Wood Press 2002)

3:59.4
The Quest for the Four-Minute Mile
(The Parrs Wood Press 2004)